Reaching *the* Next Generation

A Leading Mechanech's Time-Tested Insights for Parents and Teachers

Reaching *the* Next Generation

A Leading Mechanech's Time-Tested
Insights for Parents and Teachers

Rabbi Shmuel Yaakov Klein

Menucha Publishers

Menucha Publishers, Inc.
© 2015 by Menucha Publishers
Typeset and designed by Gittel Kaplan

All rights reserved

ISBN 978-1-61465-112-3

No part of this publication may be translated, reproduced, stored in a retrieval system, or transmitted in any form or by any means, electronic, mechanical, photocopying, recording, or otherwise, without prior permission in writing from both the copyright holder and the publisher.

Published and distributed by:
Menucha Publishers, Inc.
250 44th Street
Brooklyn, NY 11232
Tel/Fax: 718-232-0856
www.menuchapublishers.com
sales@menuchapublishers.com

Printed in Israel

ספר זה מוקדש כזכרון עולם

לזכר נש' אמ"ו ר' **אפרים יצחק קליין** ז"ל

אמי מורתי **ריקל** ע"ה לבית **גאלדשטיין**

מו"ח ר' **מרדכי מרזל** ז"ל

וחמותי **דבורה** ע"ה לבית **מקלר**

כולם אודים מוצלים מחורבן יהדות פולין שזכו

לדורות ישרים ומבורכים

יהא זכרם ברוך

מכתב ברכה

בס"ד

שמואל קמנצקי
Rabbi S. Kamenetsky

2018 Upland Way
Philadelphia, Pa 19131

Home: 215-473-2798
Study: 215-473-1212

בס"ד

ח' אלול, תשע"ד

ראיתי את ספרו של ידידי הרב שמואל יעקב קליין שליט"א בשם "על פי דרכו" בעניין חינוך הבנים, מצאתי בו דברים של טוב טעם ודעת. הוא ספר השקפות בחינוך ואף בחלקותיו וכולו מבוסס על דברי חז"ל ופוסקים וספרי מוסר וחסידות ממאורי התורה שבכל הדורות. בדפי הספר כלולים מאמרים של הדרכה למחנכים בהוראה וע"פ תורה וגם בעניני מציאות חרן על האב הנחוצים להורים בדורנו. הספר הוא מבצע גדול בחינוך ואין ספק שתצא ממנו תעלת רבה למעיינים בו.

ולכן ראוי לחזק ידי המחבר, הרב הנ"ל, שהוא מרתך וסופר מפורסם ואף ממנהלי תורה מסורת. ובכן הנני מברכו בברכת הצלחה רבה ושיעזור השי"ת שישכיל בכל מעשה ידי.

מכתב ברכה

בס"ד

שלמה אליהו מילר
רה"כ ואב"ד דכולל טאראנטא

פה יצא הרב הגאון יעקב הלוי שלזינגר אשר ברכו
הקב"ה בכשרונות יפים ולכבר כתב ברבה שאלתות בעיון
תולין, ולכבר נקבע לרבים לשמוח מומחה רה"ג זצ"ל בדר שלום
לתולדה אשר בחקור זאת במומחים לברר ספק דבר של
וכן שאלתי את הרב ובקש ממני ברכה על שנותי
לבנות ספר להפיץ מעין הטוב שנתן ה' לו בעמקו
בלב טבעי וחפץ ה' בידו יצלח ואמר לו
ורבים בבקשה זו ולו תחזקנו יוסף
נותן הדרבה

מכתב ברכה

ק"ק
ישיבה שערי תורה

הלל דיינוויד
1118 East 12th Street
Brooklyn, NY 11230

בכבוד ידידי הנעלה הרב ר' שמואל זייגר שליט"א

קבלנו לנכון המכתב מהוועדה בעניני חינוך והשתדל אתנו וקראנו אותו הנה וראה ונגיע להם דברים הרבה בעבודים את כלל ועם המחברת בעניינים מיוחדים כבוד של עולם כאחד. ואין ספק שהמאמרים האלו בעיהם עוזבים ממני תועלת גדולה לכל הלומד בהם.

לכן יזכו זכות הרבים יפעת היוזמים להוציא לאור המאמרים האלו ויבורך כל הרבים העוזרים על זה בזכיית דברי תורה באורך.

החתום בברכת התורה
ונאמן לתורה מן

עולמים בהנה ובגן
ד' ב'

הלל ד' ייגוויץ

CONTENTS

Acknowledgments 11
Introduction 13

PART ONE: והודעתָם לבנֶיך ולבנֵי בנֶיך
HASHKAFOS AND IDEALS WE SEEK TO IMPART

The Fragmentation of Sentiments 19
Three *Chinuch* Fundamentals 24
"Raising the Rus" in an EKM Generation 30
Milk Bottles at the Door 35
Ahavas Yisrael — An Achievable Pedagogic Goal 40
The Road to True Humility 45
Getting to Know Zushe! 50
The Quest for Refinement 55
Secular… but Not Secularism — Part One 60
Secular… but Not Secularism — Part Two 65
"Commencement" Exercises 70
Imparting *Ahavas Eretz Yisrael* 75

PART TWO: יסר בנך ויניחך ויתן מעדנים לנפשך
PEDAGOGICAL PRACTICES THAT BEAR MENTIONING

Reaching Each and Every One 85
Testing…Testing…1, 2, 3 93
A Language of the Soul 98
Iggud: Remembering Individuals within the Group 103
Friends and Not Projects 109
Chinuch Going On Vacation? 114
Happy to Be Here! 119

Upholding the Tech Vigil 124
Brandy and Cake 129
The *Chacham* Wants to Be Here! 134
More than a Replacement: A Real Father 138
In Pursuit of Excellence 144
Misbehaviors — Opportunity Knocking 149
Creating an Air of Interactivity 153
Brick by Brick 158

PART THREE: שמע בני מוסר אביך... תורת אמך
THE CRUCIAL ROLE PLAYED BY PARENTS

Singing the Tune of the Teen 165
Parenting: Instinct vs. Skill 170
It's What Fathers and Mothers Are For! 175
The Parental Portion of *Chinuch* — Part One 180
The Parental Portion of *Chinuch* — Part Two 185
The Parental Portion of *Chinuch* — Part Three 190

PART FOUR: כי היא חייך ואורך ימיך
AN ASSORTMENT OF *CHINUCH* STANDARDS AND GOALS

Lofty, Extrinsic Pursuits 197
The *Pshetl* — A Key Component 202
Inquire about Earlier Days! 207
Girls of Today… Women of Tomorrow 212
The Challenges Facing Community Schools 217
Investing Life Itself 222
The *Bas Mitzvah* "Culture" 227
A Vocation Unlike All Others 232

ACKNOWLEDGMENTS

Any occasion of an individual's achievement of note is a time for humble recognition of the *siyata d'Shemaya* that has enabled it. Ultimately nothing is brought to fruition without this.

Almost equally compelling is my need to express *hakaras hatov* to a number of individuals whose lives have somehow meshed with my own to open vistas of thought and experience, to provide sounding boards for ideas and conclusions… and to facilitate the writing endeavor that has furnished this volume of essays.

At the top of that list are the members of my immediate family whose patience and wisdom have been vital to me over the years, notwithstanding that I fail to express this regularly.

Included in these ranks are the thousands of *talmidim* with whom I interacted for three-and-a-half decades, as *rebbi*, as teacher, or as *menahel*. We are taught that *"ein chacham k'baal hanisayon,"* wisdom is the nearly exclusive byproduct of experience. On that basis, I need merely to echo the words of *Chazal*, *"U'mitalmidai yoser m'kulam"* — it is they who have taught me so much.

I have had the great fortune and *zechus* to be a writer for the English *Hamodia* since its inception in 5758/1998. For the past number of years, I have been among its cadre of *chinuch* columnists. I am thus grateful to *Hamodia*'s publisher/editor, Mrs. Ruth Lichtenstein, and her staff, for providing a most distinctive venue for the airing of many concepts appearing in this book.

I am likewise beholden to Reb Hirsch Traube and Menucha Publishers for all the assistance they have provided in the publication of *Reaching the Next Generation*.

May the *Ribbono shel Olam* grant all *arichus yamim* and continued *hatzlachah*.

INTRODUCTION

It might strike one as odd that there is no *masechta* — no tractate in the Mishnah and Gemara that is devoted to the topic of *chinuch* and all of its related sub-topics. In consideration of the complexities that are involved in Jewish education, it would appear that there should have been detailed discussion of the issues.

Here and there in the words of *Chazal* there are references to the concept of *"talmidim"* and *"melamdei tinokos,"* but even the sum total of these references does not equal a comprehensive compendium of the would-be *halachos* and traditions associated with *chinuch*.

In truth, when we explore the Rambam, the *Tur*, and the *Shulchan Aruch*, we do discover relatively detailed exposés of what is a halachically based approach to pedagogy, but in more ways than one this only underscores the notion that the rights and wrongs of *chinuch* are the subject of an evolving perspective shaped over time by the collective guidance of Torah luminaries through the ages.

So, even if we scour the pages of *Hilchos Melamdim* we may not unearth a long-standing and universally acclaimed truth regarding such issues as written tests, guidelines for homework, inclusion vs. resource room, tenure for *melamdim*, a *hashkafah* for *chinuch habanos*, and much more. This fact has provided both the opportunity and the need for investing thought into these and other crucial matters in the area of *chinuch* — to address new realities and to apply the wisdom of *Gedolei Yisrael* to them. And this, notwithstanding the fact that ours is the most historically rooted legacy of learning on earth!

The Jewish schooling tradition is a long one, rich in custom and ideology. By contrast, the history of public schooling in North America is a brief one, commencing in the first half of the nineteenth century. Its counterpart among the Jewish people traces its roots back twenty-one centuries to a *kohein gadol* by the name of Yehoshua ben Gamla, whose tenure was during the reign of King Alexander Yannai.

Yet, as Rav Yitzchak Hutner, *zt"l*, the late Rosh Yeshivah of Yeshivah Rabbeinu Chaim Berlin, pointed out, that fact ought not to be seen as a cause for pride or triumphalism. The advent of "*melamdei tinnokos*" — effectively, the Jewish school — was sourced in the failings of the Jewish home, explained Rav Hutner. The ideal paradigm of Jewish learning was for fathers to learn with sons. It was when Yehoshua ben Gamla pondered the weakness of that parenting model that he took the brilliant, precautionary initiative to ensure that Jewish children will always develop within an environment of Torah.

As the Gemara declares, if not for Yehoshua ben Gamla, the Torah would have been forgotten by the Jewish people. So, while pride may not be the appropriate emotion triggered by his *chinuch* initiative, gratitude certainly is. While Jewish education was grounded in a shortcoming in Jewish society, it has nevertheless been the spinal column of Jewish survival through our nation's odyssey in Diaspora for two millennia.

That being said, it is crucial to note that our exposure to the challenges of wandering virtually to the four corners of the world, combined with the corrosive impact from the passage of time, has created an ongoing — if not an increasingly urgent — need for an examination of *chinuch* ideals and for us to discern exactly what the Torah would have *mechanchim* do. Ambiguity in some areas of life has been the handmaiden of *galus*.

On the one hand, the word "*mesorah*," tradition, has thus come to mean many distinct things for different communities. This is an example of the dispersion factor.

On the other hand there is the time factor. The Kotzker Rebbe, *zy"a*, explained the verse, "*Binu shenos dor vador*," by reminding us that "*shenos*" is connected in its denotation, to the word "*shinui*," which means "change." He thus suggested that what the Torah is urging is that we shall understand the ways in which one generation changes from its preceding generations. Each era offers new realities and thus necessitates new strategies. It thus behooves us all — whether we are parents or classroom educators — to reconsider the pedagogical techniques and truisms that we have been likely to take for granted.

This is what precipitated *Reaching the Next Generation*, which offers a broad sampling of issues and possible perspectives regarding them. It is my fervent hope and *tefillah* that the chapters before you will help to shed at least a marginal ray of light upon some matters that lie at the heart of *chinuch habanim v'habanos*.

PART ONE

והודעתם לבניך ולבני בניך

דברים ד:ט

HASHKAFOS AND IDEALS
WE SEEK TO IMPART

THE FRAGMENTATION OF SENTIMENTS

So you go to the toy store and buy a one thousand piece puzzle. Excitedly, you bring it home, open it up and are about to begin the challenging task of assembly when you decide to count the pieces beforehand. To your chagrin, you discover that there are 100 pieces missing. Here is the question: do you resign yourself to the shortage because, after all, the puzzle is ninety percent whole (and ninety percent is not bad!)? Or, do you conclude that the lack of ten percent of the pieces makes the entire puzzle fundamentally problematic? If you were to choose the second of these responses, you would certainly not be alone.

Oddly, though, when it comes to bringing up children correctly *al pi Torah*, we often opt for the first.

With the plethora of information and activities — curricular and extra-curricular — to which our children have access, one of the dangers that presents itself in the contemporary world of *chinuch* is the fragmentation of sentiments. In other words, a modern-day challenge we face in educating our young is the need to infuse a complete cognitive perspective in accordance with Torah and Yiddishkeit. The composite — the "puzzle," so to speak — is incomplete without it.

The Chafetz Chaim commented that if even the slightest aspect of an individual's totality is not in sync with a patently Jewish mindset, there is a question about whether or not his morning recitation of the *berachah* of "*She'lo asani goy*" might not be *l'vatalah*. A person cannot with equanimity bless Hashem for His having made him or her a Jew if there is even the smallest element of his being that is "non-Jewish," so to speak, said the Chafetz Chaim.

What everything essentially boils down to is the question of what commands a person's loyalties. Every day we recite in *Krias Shema* the dictate that we shall love Hashem with all our hearts. One of Rashi's explanations of this notion ("*b'chol levavcha*") is that a Jew's heart shall not be "*chaluk al HaMakom* — divided against Hashem." And while that seems to suggest that a Jew must not "dispute" anything that is in Torah, that suggestion alone truly borders on the obvious and needs not be stated. The intent, then, is perhaps that a person's *loyalty* to Hashem must not be less than absolute and all-pervasive. In the same way that we would surely scoff at a person who claimed to be Torah observant half a week and non-observant the other half, we ought to realize that it is almost as absurd for one to say that he or she is obedient to Hashem in most — but not all — aspects of his life — including his *thinking*. The only difference is that the former is a vertical split, so to speak, while the latter is horizontal. Both are equally wrong.

Curiously, however, the latter has gained tacit approval among the faithful. People are usually willing to accept, and even to "understand," an observant person who has adopted values that come from beyond the parameters of our *mesorah*.

Several years ago I heard a comment made by one of the most venerated *mechanchim* in the contemporary North America Bais Yaakov movement. "We are producing a generation of young people who are more *frum* than their predecessors, but also less Jewish!" he claimed.

What he meant was that the efforts at teaching our *talmidim* and *talmidos* all aspects of halachah, including the broad range of precautions and stringencies, is meeting with success, while we may simultaneously be failing to inculcate *sheleimus*, that is, a Jewish *weltanschauung* and a Jewish self-concept into those same *talmidim* and *talmidos*. In other words, one of the possible failings in the overall *chinuch* picture is that it remains possible for our children to emerge from their Jewish schooling with a fragmentation of sentiments.

This is not to say, *chas v'shalom*, that the bid to impart the details of halachah to students is in any way lacking merit; for, on the contrary, it is meritorious indeed. It does, however, point to a glaring incongruity between heightened "halachah sense" on the one hand and decreased "Jewish-self-concept sense" on the other.

It is therefore important to consider a number of devices that can be used, both in the school and in the home, to avoid — and possibly even to correct — this wrong.

1. Obviously at the very top of the list is the need to shelter children from the insidiousness of the media and of pop culture. Alternatively, so much emphasis has been placed in the world of *chinuch* on the battles against television and Internet in the recent past that it needs not be reiterated here in any detail.

2. Certainly, near the top of the list would be a directive pronounced by the *Nesivos Shalom*, among others. This is to teach youngsters the fundamentals of *emunah* and *bitachon* — articles of faith — over and over again. Stories that emphasize *hashgachah pratis* (Divine Providence), for instance, are particularly effective, avers the Slonimer Rebbe,

zt"l, in shaping the sentiments of a young person to be in keeping with Jewish *sheleimus*. The important thing is to constantly stress the ways in which the Creator is always involved in our lives.

And the time for imparting the vital messages of *emunah u'vitachon* does not begin "later on," when children have grown into adolescents, and when a mindset is much harder to structure, but rather when they are very young. The topic must be included alongside of *kriah*, *haschalas Chumash*, and *haschalas Gemara*.

3. Children ought not to be misled into thinking that their external Jewish appearance is unimportant. When a child sees his own image — either in a mirror or reflected in his classmates — he must see a distinctly Jewish entity, for that which is essentially different must look different too. Uniforms for girls' schools and a specific dress code for boys are useful tools. (The effectiveness of these things, though, must not be undermined by our children's mode of dress on off-school days.)

In *Zera Kodesh*, the Ropshitzer Rebbe claims that the facilitator to Yaakov Avinu's ability to deceive his father was Eisav's clothing. The Eisav-like appearance impacted upon Yaakov's very essence. In the same way, a traditionally Jewish appearance (whatever that means, specifically) will contribute to a child's Jewish essence.

4. Related to the previous point is the need to train children to speak "Jewishly," for speech both reveals one's thoughts and shapes them. The merit of Egyptian Jewry before *Yetzias Mitzrayim*, whereby they did not change their original ethnic "'tongue," certainly means that their style of speech — let alone their actual language — remained

distinctly Jewish. Today, varied and seemingly innocuous colloquialisms, originating from the proverbial "street," have infiltrated into our children's nomenclature. While these are perhaps not classified as *nivul peh* (hopefully), they do nevertheless paint Jewish speech with non-Jewish hues. That, too, compromises the *sheleimus* of young people.

So, with the heightened awareness that has surrounded the theme of *shemiras halashon* over the last few decades, there ought to be emphasis not only on what we say, but on how we say it.

The truth is that the list of elements to be addressed in an attempt to promote wholeness in our children's Jewish commitment is almost endless. Indeed, that is exactly what the definition of *sheleimus* is: it includes everything. The above, then, is merely a sampling of issues. The common thread, however, lies in maintaining the desired focus: the assurance that everything our children do and think is in keeping with the behavior and the philosophy of devout Jews.

No, there is no disputing that as beautiful as our puzzles can be, their potential can be realized only if all — not most — of the pieces are in the box.

THREE CHINUCH FUNDAMENTALS

Not long ago I had occasion to address the parent body of a prominent Brooklyn yeshivah. During a question period, I was asked what the most fundamental aspect of *chinuch* is. In terms of the breadth of that query's scope, it is the classically "impossible" question to answer, as there are so many components. At the same time, it did prompt me to focus on a number of specifics.

BEGINNINGS

Certainly a connotation of a concept cannot be entertained without a prior understanding of its denotation. Therefore, when one speaks of *chinuch* one necessarily speaks also of the "beginning of a process." We read (*Bereishis* 14:14) that when Avraham Avinu heard that he must come to his nephew Lot's rescue, "*Vayarek es chanichav* — He led forth those whom he had trained." On the word "*chanichav*," Rashi points out that the expression means a person — or an instrument — *starting* to perform the task that he, or it, is destined to perform in the future.

Elsewhere (*Devarim* 20:5) Rashi states, "*Kol chinuch lashon haschalah* — All forms of the word '*chinuch*' signify a beginning."

Consider, then, that our designation of "*chinuch*" as the term for Jewish education dates back to Shlomo HaMelech and to the oft-cited *pasuk*, "*Chanoch lana'ar al pi darko*" (*Mishlei* 22:6). What this means, then, is that the backbone of Jewish education is the notion that a child who learns Torah is only beginning to do so — and that he will, in a sense, forever remain a "child learning Torah." With the process being never-ending, schooling for a young Yid must be portrayed as nothing but the beginning of that lifelong endeavor. If we impart to children that only a specific core curriculum must be "covered" and when that is done the objective is complete, we fail to inculcate into that child the crucial message that *chinuch* is only a *haschalah*. A child must feel that he has never completed the task. Even when a *siyum* is celebrated, it is predicated upon a "*hadran*," upon the notion of starting all over again.

So, if we can assume that a person's aspirations are what define his essence, it follows that by cultivating such aspirations as more learning, deeper *yiras Shamayim*, more stringency in the performance of *mitzvos* — the backbone of *chinuch* will be in the hearts of *talmidim*.

CHARACTER DEVELOPMENT

A second fundamental is based on what the starting point of *chinuch* needs to be. In *Parashas Yisro* (*Shemos* 18:21) the Torah describes the qualities necessary for *Klal Yisrael*'s spiritual leaders to have. In his commentary on that *pasuk*, Rabbeinu Bachaye writes, "Come see how great is the power of sterling character. The *tzaddikim* in the Torah, such as Noach, Avraham and Yaakov, were not lauded for their intelligence and wisdom, but rather for being '*tamim*,' that is, for their *middos*. Also Moshe was praised for his humility."

In *chinuch* one must seek first and foremost to infuse classical

Jewish personality traits into children as a foundation for Jewish learning. Rabbeinu Bachaye concludes, "This is all to teach us that the main aspect is not the wisdom but the straightness of character, in the same way that the fruit — and not the trunk — is the primary feature of the tree."

Rav Eliyahu Dessler writes on the practical aspect of *middos* training in *chinuch habanim* (see *Michtav Me'Eliyahu* vol. 3, pp. 360-1). In discussing some pertinent mistakes that have seeped into the Torah world and that have been generated by post-modern and psychology-based educational theorists, Rav Dessler writes, "They think that one needs to develop independence in children. This is a terrible mistake. It is not independence that we need to develop in children, but rather submission. Even if we will develop humility and submission in a child he will learn arrogance and aggression on his own. So, to actually teach a child to feel, 'I and none other!' is tantamount to teaching him the law of Edom, the rule of selfishness and dishonesty."

Although it is undoubtedly virtuous to teach a student to be academically independent and innovative in his thinking, character matters are a different story altogether. According to Rav Dessler, a road that is paved with an inflated sense of self is a road that leads to spiritual ruin.

In *Nesivei Chinuch* (ch. 7, section 3) the Slonimer Rebbe cites a related thought elucidated by Reb Chaim Vital in his *Shaarei Kedushah*: It is interesting to note that although the Creator bears great disdain for those with poor personal attributes — for instance *Chazal* teach that one who is quick to anger or one who is arrogant is likened unto an idol-worshiper — nevertheless the issue of poor *middos* is not actually spoken about openly in the Torah. The reason for this, explained R' Chaim Vital, is that the very pursuit of Torah itself is founded upon one's having worked at the perfection of his *middos* beforehand. Indeed Torah was given to those who are essentially Jewish, he continued, and one who has not sought to first develop his *middos* lacks a proper Jewish essence. It is a prior prerequisite to Torah and therefore not part of Torah, explained the Slonimer Rebbe.

To be sure, in an age such as ours, when we are surrounded by a culture that inadvertently promotes personality weaknesses, such as self-centeredness, the need for *middos* training becomes even more pronounced for our yeshivos. Even in the secular world there is today an increasing awareness of such school trends as bullying and as cliques among students. A yeshivah's failure to deal with these things is a most serious failing indeed.

INTERNALIZATION

Perhaps the most crucial pillar of all is that we should teach so as to infuse truth and piety into the hearts of *talmidim*. In the annals of Chassidus it is taught that after having soaked in the Chassidus of Kotzk for a long time — much to the initial chagrin of his father Rav Shlomo Eiger — Reb Leibeleh Eiger (who later would become Lubliner Rebbe) paid a visit to his most illustrious grandfather Rav Akiva Eiger. "What did you learn in Kotzk?" asked the *Zeide*.

"I learned that there is a Creator in Heaven," Reb Leibeleh answered. At that point Rav Akiva Eiger summoned the housekeeper and asked her who created the world. She said, "The Creator." Rav Akiva then challenged his grandson, "Even the housekeeper says that there is a Creator." To this the grandson replied, "She says it, but I have learned to feel it!"

Arguably, one might need to spend time in a Kotzk in order to internalize Yiddishkeit. At the same time, Rav Moshe Feinstein, in a famous *teshuvah* (*Igros Moshe*, Y.D. 3, *siman* 71) writes, "It is imperative that the teacher, when teaching Torah, ensures that the *talmid* accepts what is taught so much that he realizes in his heart and soul that this is the fundamental of life and the true purpose of man in the world." Even without Kotzk, it is attainable.

If there is no internalization, there is no real *chinuch*, despite that there may be academic, secular-style, learning. For us, education is *avodas hakodesh,* an undertaking of sacredness — not a dry and mundane transmission of material and ideas.

1. Of course, one must seek the tools to facilitate internalization. *Tefillah* is a vital focus. Of course, there is much more. For instance, the Brisker Rav used to emphasize the importance of *sippurei tzaddikim*, telling children stories of the lives of Torah luminaries. When children are constantly urged to emulate such role models — in particular as we are relentlessly accosted, as it were, by a world in which sports figures and entertainers are all but worshiped by society at large — that emulation becomes an important goal, and goals form our essence.

2. Rav Dessler (*Michtav Me'Eliyahu* vol. 3, p. 161) encourages educators to constantly appeal to the Creator's role in our lives, through mention of such phrases, as, "*b'ezras Hashem*," "*im yirtzeh Hashem*" and so on. The subliminal reminders of Hashem's role in our lives will prompt students to internalize what we teach, and it will strengthen the *emunah* that our children need to develop.

3. Needless to say, Torah study itself is a mighty force in internalization. The *Avnei Neizer* used to say in the name of his father-in-law, the Kotzker Rebbe, that a *blatt* of Gemara purifies one just as a *mikveh*, which engulfs one completely, does (see *Siach Sarfei Kodesh* — on Torah).

4. It is very possible, however, that these words were spoken in a time when there was first a firm footing in *Torah she'biksav*. It is typical today, however, that once Ge-

mara becomes the major focus for yeshivah students, their study of Chumash — perhaps never adequately pursued in younger grades — is all but forgotten. Chumash, apart from being a *limud* that is obviously important on its own right — teaches lessons of *emunah,* the concept of role models, and the part that *HaKadosh Baruch Hu* plays in our lives, more powerfully than all else. It is a perfect instrument for internalization.

I would not be so trite as to suggest that this encompasses the *hashkafah* of *chinuch*. I would submit, though, that these three ideas do for a solid bedrock upon which *chinuch* can be built.

"RAISING THE RUS" IN AN EKM GENERATION

R' Ze'ira's words, cited in *Midrash Rus Rabbah*, ring out a timeless message. This Megillah contains no statements of practical halachah, nothing of what is forbidden or permitted, neither of what is clean or unclean, he declares. Why then was it written, he asks. His answer: it was written with the purpose of teaching how great is the reward for *gomlei chasadim*, those who perform acts of kindness.

As to how that conclusion emerges: Rus was a paragon of the virtue of *chesed*; therefore she was rewarded with the destiny that Jewish monarchy, including the long-awaited dominion of *Melech HaMashiach*, would emanate from her progeny. Now, the premise that a Megillah must teach practical halachah in order for it to be written is interesting enough. What is even more impacting, however, is the idea that the sole purpose of the story of Rus is to illustrate the importance of *chesed*.

The level on which that is most curious indeed relates, with irony, to her *yichus*, her family lineage. While she may have been of royal stock, the daughter of King Eglon, she was also a scion of a nation recorded in the Torah for its notoriety. Moav, eternally distanced from the gene pool of the Jewish people, was guilty of "*asher lo kidmu eschem balechem u'vamayim.*" When the Jewish nation approached, weary and hungry from their travels, Moav failed to offer it even the barest of sustenance — bread and water. The nation of Rus acted with a decided lack of *chesed*; therefore they were ignominiously branded as forever unworthy of marriage within the Jewish nation — at least, as far as their males were concerned.

In truth, there are many interpretations of the sins of Moav that resulted in their becoming *issurei biah*, "forbidden from coming" into our fold. However, among the *baalei mussar*, what is emphasized is that a people weak in *chesed* cannot be linked to a people who thrive on that very tradition. That is the extent to which kindness plays a role of prominence in our lives.

This, then, is the irony surrounding Rus: a product of the selfish and unkind society of Moav unfolds in Jewish history as a unique exemplar of selflessness and kindness, even to the extent of her deserving to be the matriarch of our *malchus*. She must have been a veritable tower of fortitude to have been able to overcome the negative influences of her environment, and all this while excelling in both modesty and religious devotion.

Parents would certainly be eager to discover the secret recipe for producing and raising a Rus in their own children — if only it were possible!

It seems almost certain, however, that Rus was an anomaly — a *tzadeikes* not *because* of the way she was reared but *despite* it. She was not a product of her education, but rather an antithesis to it. But we can neither aspire to raising anomalies nor to having good children through their "rebounding" from our flawed *chinuch*, as did Rus. So, is there in fact anything practical regarding the *chinuch* of our children that we might learn from the story of Rus?

R' Ze'ira felt that there is. While not generating conventional, practical, *halachic* prescriptions, the Megillah does come to teach us a lesson, he averred. It is a message about *chesed* being rewarded with noble offspring. It is message of the need to internalize *chesed* and to convey that concept of kindness to our children.

The crux of raising a Rus, in a nutshell, is being able to instill in our children gentleness of bearing and sensitivity to others. Yet, it often seems that those dispositions are going the way of the rotary-dial telephone and the neighborhood milkman. In a climate where an aggressive nature seems to stand an individual in better stead than an *eidel* one, producing a Rus becomes all the more difficult. In an environment where expediency takes precedence over scruples and where "having" is more envied than "being," raising a Rus becomes all but an impossible dream.

Alternatively, that must be the message of the Megillah. If Rus developed in spite of her environment, we are able to help our children to acquire the same ideal traits of character, and, as with Rus, in spite of our environment. But how?

We live in an EKM age. "*Es Kumt Mir*," I deserve it. Years ago I noticed an advertisement for a particular product, in which the consumer looks out and says, "It may cost more, but I deserve it!" Back then, I genuinely failed to understand on what basis the person in the ad made the determination that he or she deserved that — or anything else for that matter. The answer, I found out, lay in the unwritten credo of our age. "I deserve it" is the slogan of the contemporary environment. "*Es kumt mir*." Deservingness is now generated by desire.

This mood has seriously encroached into the lives of Torah

Jews, such that it is as prevalent among us as among anyone. When today's child "wants" something, parents rush to provide it: a new toy, a new item of clothing, a treat — almost anything. Consequently, children have become accustomed to thinking that their mere wanting something justifies their receiving it. As a result of that lack of parental discretion, today's child has blamelessly internalized the concept of *Es kumt mir*.

In *Yoreh Dei'ah*, there is a rule, "*Eidi d'tarach l'miflat lo bola* — when meat discharges fluid, it will not absorb," for the direction of movement is contrary to absorption. The same holds true in the reverse. If absorption is occurring, discharging cannot occur simultaneously. This notion applies to all of nature, including human nature. If one is exclusively predisposed to absorbing, to receiving, to acquiring, he will have a most difficult time giving, helping, and seeing the needs of others.

The EKM age is thus antithetical to fostering kindness and *chesed* in our youth.

What Boaz noticed about Rus was her demeanor. Her modesty, her gentleness, and, as Rashi points out, that she gathered from the *leket* in a manner which showed consideration. When he later learned that she was gathering for her aging mother-in-law, his relative, he was even further impressed. What we might also bear in mind, however, is that she started life as a princess: it must have been humbling indeed for her to gather leftovers like a pauper. Yet, as the Malbim points out, she did this willingly in order to ensure that her mother-in-law would not need to.

Rus rose to the point of overcoming what surely was the EKM air, to which she could have been legitimately entitled. She became able to rule over herself, a fact that rendered her singularly suited to being the mother of Jewish monarchs, of the rulers of *Klal Yisrael*.

Yes, our children can perhaps transcend, as Rus did, the contingencies of EKM, which is the bane of our times. But, if it were to happen, it would border on the miraculous. What is much more certain to happen is that by our catering to our children's every whim and by pandering to their distorted sense of deservingness, we are making it nearly impossible to raise a Rus.

Let us learn from the message of R' Ze'ira and resolve to teach our children, at least on occasion, that *"Es kumt mir nisht!"*

MILK BOTTLES AT THE DOOR

On a recent trip to London, I noted that each morning a fresh bottle of milk was left at the stoop at the entrance to my host's house. I was nostalgically thrown back to a different land and a different clime — to the Toronto of my childhood, when the morning milk delivery was a common occurrence. Some might recall that houses were once built with an easy-to-open "milk box" near one of its exterior doors for this very purpose.

Yes, in London the bottle was now plastic instead of the glass of yesteryear; and the milk was *chalav Yisrael*, which was not necessarily the case back then; but the practice of leaving a bottle of milk in front of the house smacked of times long gone, of days when trust and gentleness of character were the order of the day.

Something tells me that North American readers under fifty years of age may not even know what I am referring to. "What? Leave a bottle of milk out in the open? In Brooklyn? It'll be stolen within five minutes!"

Well, maybe so, and I would not necessarily actually suggest that the practice be reintroduced. What I am getting at, however, is that the small milk bottle, boldly standing there in the morning fog collecting the London dew was for me a throwback to a kinder, gentler time.

That is when nostalgia gave way to puzzlement over what has become of us.

I have often wondered what it is in our changing world that has precipitated deterioration in the social mood that permeates our lives. What is it that has all but eliminated the mild-mannered demeanor of times gone by; what has transformed us into callous and aggressive beings?

While the answer is not simple, I would suggest that the prosperity with which we have been blessed is one component that has taken its toll. In the famous opening chapter of *Mesillas Yesharim*, Rav Moshe Chaim Luzzatto speaks of the various challenges that veritably surround us on all sides. Both poverty and wealth pose challenges, he avers, citing the haunting words of Shlomo HaMelech (*Mishlei* 30:9). "*Pen esba v'kichashti v'amarti mi Hashem* — Lest I become satiated and deny, saying, 'Who is Hashem'… *pen ivaresh v'ganavti* — or lest I become impoverished and steal." Whether a person is afflicted with the hardship of poverty or graced with the mixed blessing of prosperity, he is tested spiritually, for on the one hand he may steal and on the other he may deny his Creator.

Let us consider the distinction, though, between those two tests. Theft is undeniably both a sin against Hashem and a crime against another person, but it does not necessarily bespeak a seriously innate character flaw. It does not indicate that the individual has become someone else: it only shows that he has succumbed to the pressing needs of his situation and committed the indiscretion. One can return what he has stolen to its owner, repent, and be back on his way, so to speak.

Wealth and prosperity, on the other hand, have the power to transform the very essence of the individual. The transformation that can result from affluence and success affects the very core of the individual. I would add, however, that it is not merely the affluence itself that will impact on him: it is the pursuit of affluence, and it is living in a society where that pursuit is touted as primary and supremely worthy.

Moreover, I would add that the core-changing transformation is not in any way restricted to relationships that are *"bein adam laMakom,"* between man and Hashem, but perhaps even more so they impact significantly on the relationships that are *bein adam lachaveiro*, interpersonal.

In other words, the way we interact with others often indicates the sentiment, "Don't mess with me, and don't get in my way, because I am busy trying to make my fortune." The result is that others become devalued in the individual's eyes. He has no compunctions rushing through the open door that you have opened — before you get the chance to. And no "excuse me," or "thank you" to boot! He has no problem taking your right of way away from you on the road, because he needs to get where he is going quickly. He has nothing compelling him to say good morning or *Gut Shabbos* to you, because other people in general are not that important in his scheme of things. *Hakaras hatov* may be a nice feeling to express, but he is not that interested in doing so, because he is too busy to consider *your* feelings. And the list goes on and on.

In fact, stop and consider the common line of questions that emerges in today's *shidduch* scene. Is the girl/boy an academic whiz? Is the girl/boy *lebedik*? Is his/her father a man of means? What does he do for a living? What is her dress size? Is she pretty? What seminary did she attend? Does he dress up-to-date? Is he handsome? Does he have red hair? Which Brisk did he learn in? Now, while I would not go quite to the extent of suggesting that these (or some of these) questions have absolutely no place within the *shidduch* "resume," I would say that I have not heard often enough that people ask about the prospective candidate's *middos*, his or her character as far as sincerity is concerned. Have we ever been asked about a *bachur*, "Does he *daven ehrlich*?"

The society in which we live has grown increasingly goal-oriented, but with the added aspect that the goals in question are more and more crass and this-worldly. The toll that all this has taken on the position that *middos* and *derech eretz* occupies on our lives is sadly enormous.

A related component that has become disproportionately emphasized in contemporary Jewish life is, as already noted, academic accomplishment. Without downplaying Torah study, I suggest that we dare not lose sight of the fact that, as *Chazal* have taught, *middos* and *derech eretz* are prerequisites for Torah ("*kadmah laTorah*"). And though parents and *mechanchim* alike pay dutiful lip service to that frequently cited *maamar*, the reality is that academics alone are almost exclusively rewarded in our society and in our schools. Isn't it the sharpest *bachur* or the biggest *masmid* who is welcomed into the yeshivos of his choice? And isn't it the most studious young lady, with the highest grades, who is the one admitted into the "best" seminaries? Genuine *baalei middos* are not quite as fortunate. (And although I grant that academic achievement must surely remain a key element, should character not at least form part of the equation for admittance?)

Similarly, in the broad sphere of secular education, as well as in our own more restricted world of *chinuch*, issues such as "bullying" have come to enjoy the limelight recently. Studies show that there is now a higher incidence of schoolyard victimization than there has been in the past. This includes physical, verbal, and emotional bullying. It affects both genders almost equally, and it traverses all demographic lines. While we Yidden tend to harbor distaste for the term "bullying," because of the nasty aura of that word, the issue itself is nevertheless a known concern in our circles as much as anywhere else. How many yeshivah parents have children who are on either the giving end or the receiving end of this low-level "terrorism," (if one may use that phrase!) being played out each day in our yeshivos? As an educator, I dealt with countless instances of children being afraid to come to school in the morning for fear of one sort of bullying or another.

Time for a reality check! Essentially human nature is the same as when the *Ribbono shel Olam* created mankind; it would likely be incorrect to postulate that people are really more aggressive and unkind today than they used to be. What is more plausible, though, is that societal changes have created this outward effect. There is presently a premium placed — almost exclusively — upon *tachlis*, tangible achievement, as opposed to character refinement.

It is the role of today's educator — parent and *mechanech* alike — to counteract this — in the way we carry ourselves, in the role modeling we present to our young charges and in the redistribution of emphasis that is applied to what we teach — and how we teach it.

To be perfectly truthful, while in London I was invited to give a workshop on how to handle the issue of bullying to the *rebbeim* of a particular yeshivah. It seems that morning milk-bottle delivery has no real bearing on the level of *middos* that is manifest in any community. Alternatively my bout of nostalgia was not for the milk bottle: it was for heightened *menschlichkeit* of once upon a time. And that does need a boost.

AHAVAS YISRAEL — AN ACHIEVABLE PEDAGOGIC GOAL

I n the contemporary world of *chinuch* there is mounting concern among schools about the need to discover the best formula for turning out the most accomplished *talmidim* and *talmidos*. In trying to meet the noble objectives of imparting a healthy work ethic and proper learning skills, and of transmitting a massive volume of Torah knowledge with true comprehension, one area is frequently and sorely overlooked. Indeed, one would be hard put to find a *mosad Torah* where this issue is actually included in its syllabus of study. At the same time, if asked, not a single *mechanech* would deny the supreme importance of this topic. It is "*ahavas Yisrael*."

People tend to pay lip service to this sublime ideal. Yet, arguably, there is too little promotion of it within our yeshivos. In truth, in larger communities, where there are many *mosdos Torah*, the atmosphere within the world of *chinuch* tends to be more sectarian and parochial. And while there are certainly many advantages to such a scenario of educational "choices" being provided by a range of yeshivos, there are also challenges that arise from it. For example, the inculcation of *ahavas Yisrael* into *talmidim* becomes more problematic, since the mood of exclusion in which children are nurtured can go contrary to it. At the same time, in terms of a syllabus of study, the challenge might exist for everyone equally.

To be sure, in the general non-Jewish world of education, no ideal that might be considered the equivalent of *ahavas Yisrael* is promoted. Indeed, the notion doesn't really even exist. Yes, there might be a premium placed on patriotism in the school agendas of some nations. But that is an entirely different concept: that is devotion to a state or to a national heritage — not to people *per se*. *Ahavas Yisrael*, on the other hand, is the love for and devotion to people who are co-religionists. This is notably unique.

Consider the words of one of our people's champions of *chinuch* from the previous generation: the Slonimer Rebbe, *zy"a*. The *Nesivos Shalom* writes, "It is a general rule that Jewish education is different in a most innate way from all other types of education that exist among the nations of the world. They operate using the range of natural strengths that have been infused into the human being... Pure Jewish education, however, utilizes strengths that are supernatural, because within the Jewish child there resides a Divine element from Above..." (*Nesivei Chinuch*, Part 1).

It is reasonable, then, that just as the nature of *chinuch* is unique, so, too, might be at least a portion of — if not all of — its objectives. Content, academic and social skills do not suffice for young Jews. Our *talmidim* are incomplete if they are lacking a passion for other Yidden. Sadly, this is a deficiency in many *chinuch* situations.

Yet, rather than to discuss the reasons that the theme of *ahavas Yisrael* tends to be ignored in most schools, let us divert our attention to possible ways of imparting this ideal.

It is worth stating that frontal *mussar* — or preachments — have limited impact upon young *talmidim*, even if they can be effective with adolescents. For the pupils of elementary school age, more concrete techniques will be necessary.

- Role playing is a time-honored approach to building character. We are well aware of the Gemara in *Kiddushin* that states that the virtue of Torah learning is that it is *"meivi li'dei maaseh,"* that it facilitates action. Hence, when we wish to teach about *ahavas Yisrael*, it is obvious that acts that personify the ideal will have their impact. Doing *chesed* can go a long way towards infusing love for a fellow Jew; yet the focus on *chesed* in and of itself is slightly different. Collecting funds for such causes as Tashbar, Yad and Lev L'Achim, among others, is greatly urged for teaching *chesed*, while it may be too abstract for teaching *ahavas Yisrael*. A child benefits from having something more tangible than the raising of money upon which to focus. For instance, a program of writing letters to children in Eretz Yisrael who may have been personally touched by the tragedies of terrorism, *Rachmana litzlan*, is an extremely effective device, and there are numerous organizations that facilitate this. In addition to the genuine benefit forthcoming to the letter recipients, the writers sense a connection to real people; they experience the sensation of being *"nosei b'ol im chaveiro,"* empathy, a peripheral type of role playing. This is the bedrock of *ahavas Yisrael*.

- Another scenario, although challenging in some ways, offers a phenomenal opportunity for empathy and for *ahavas Yisrael*. There are — surely in almost all communities — children who are physically handicapped and for whom regular classroom life is almost a distant dream. Yet, there have been successful experiments by which such children have been integrated into classrooms of regularly endowed children — at least for a portion of the program. Again, the benefits are double. In addition to providing an experience and a venue for a challenged youth that will meaningfully change his or her entire life, the *mechanech* who introduces a "class project" of this sort will have given his young charges an unparalleled lesson in loving and caring for another Yid. Indeed, the reported accounts of these endeavors have shared the observation that children rise to the occasion in a tremendous way. They, too, are changed for life.

- While there certainly are numerous other similar-minded activities that will achieve the desired goal of *ahavas Yisrael*, in this context I particularly emphasize one approach. If employed correctly, it will achieve the desired objectives while simultaneously attaining a number of others as well. After all, our original goal was to discover something that can be included in an actual syllabus of learning. I refer here to teaching about the *churban* of European Jewry during the Second World War. It is content-oriented; it is certainly ideal as a unit in a history program in middle schools and high schools. And the crucial benefit is achieved whereby our sons and daughters will learn about this vital and multi-faceted topic correctly — *al pi Torah*.

Yet, despite all the other benefits it is a powerful device in heightening *ahavas Yisrael*. Consider the following. The Novominsker Rebbe, in a Rosh Chodesh Av, 5760 address to Torah Umesorah's Planning Conference on Teaching *Churban Europa*, said, "Many people feel that the most important thing is to understand the *hashkafah* of the *churban* of *Klal Yisrael*. Why did it happen? What does it mean? And so forth. There is something, however, that comes before that. Far more important than the sensitive subject of '*Mah zos asah Hashem lanu*' is to have the young growing *bnei Torah* be '*mitz'ta'er b'tzarasam shel Yisrael*', to have a feeling that as a part of *Klal Yisrael* they must shed a tear for *Klal Yisrael*'s suffering and losses."

In fact, over the past decade or so, great inroads have been made in *mosdos* around the world in broaching this crucial subject material. *Gedolei Yisrael* have given their support to the recent initiatives. In my own experience, I have found it to be a great facilitator of *ahavas Yisrael*.

No treatment of the topic of imparting *ahavas Yisrael* to our youth — even a cursory treatment such as this — can be complete without mentioning that even the most concerted and structured efforts to realize this goal are easily undermined by a feature common in the environment in which our progeny is raised. This is when the adults who occupy that environment jointly with our children allow themselves to freely express disdain for others. That yeshivah, that *chassidus*, that shul, that Bais Yaakov, that community, that *shtiebel* — that anything! So-called responsible adults, whether in the home or in the classroom, are often oblivious to the damage they cause with their casual words of derision directed at others.

We are wise to remember that *ahavas Yisrael*, like so many other precious things, can be quite fragile.

THE ROAD TO TRUE HUMILITY

A universally known truth in the realm of *middos tovos* is that *gaavah* — arrogance — is a bad personality trait. The Rambam writes (*Hilchos Dei'os* 2:5) that although one should strive towards the middle path in most characteristics, this is not so with arrogance. "*Govah haleiv*," a synonym for *gaavah*, is a trait from which one should distance himself to the extreme, the Rambam writes.

A second universally known truth — from the realm of *chinuch* — is that one of the goals to be pursued by the *mechanech* is guidance of his *talmidim* in developing *middos tovos*. The reasoning is simple: the concern of the *mechanech* must be for the complete child — and *middos* is obviously a key component of a person's *sheleimus*.

What follows from the above pair of premises is that a *mechanech* should attempt to train his *talmid* to be humble. The question that needs to be addressed, however, is how that goal can be achieved. Needless to say, speaking about the importance of *anivus* will not suffice, because such matters need to be cultivated — not simply taught. How is this achieved?

Perhaps, however, we should begin with how that goal is *not* to be achieved. Ironically, the most improper way to make a child humble was also popular once upon a time: That was to actively humble — or humiliate — him. One might suppose that "putting a child in his place" will surely teach him humility. The irony, though, is that instead of fostering *anivus*, it fosters the reverse. Putting the child down will only cause him pain. That approach, apart from the ethical issues raised by it, makes the child focus on his pain and on himself in general. Self-centeredness — even of such a negative variety — is antithetical to humility.

At the beginning of the sixth chapter of his *Nesivei Chinuch*, the Slonimer Rebbe writes, "The most successful kind of *chinuch* occurs if the *mechanech*'s methods of impacting are positive ones… and only if the image of the *mechanech* in the eyes of the child or the adolescent is not of one who frightens or of one who is interested in depriving him of basic pleasures or his imagined happiness. Rather, it should be of one who seeks to provide him with true light and spiritual pleasure." In other words, when the persona of the rebbi or *morah* generates negativity — be it fear, deprivation or, as in our context, embarrassment — good *chinuch* is not likely to occur.

One experience from my childhood years sticks in my memory, and will likely linger there forever. It was in a year where my academic performance was not stellar. For reasons I would never attribute to anyone but myself, I learned very little for a period of a few months and I knew I had to change. When I finally determined that I wanted to rise from dismal underachievement, I knew that I would have to make a bold move. One day I courageously asked the *rebbi* a question on what we were learning. He was a well-loved rebbi, hardly worthy of criticism as a rule. That said, though, that day he responded with, "Klein, don't ask me *klotz kashos*." I have no doubt that it indeed was a "*klotz kasheh*," but I am equally certain that his reaction put a damper on my readiness to take any further chances. (Come to think of it, I doubt that the phrase "*klotz kasheh*" even belongs in any classroom nomenclature to begin with.)

The goal of achieving humility will ideally be pursued by the individual for and by himself — and never forced upon him by another person.

In his commentary on *Parashas Bamidbar*, the *Sifsei Kohein* (*Shach*) explains why *Shevet Levi* was assigned the task of carrying the Mishkan even before they were counted. Had they first learned about their diminutive number, as compared to the other *shevatim*, they would have felt sadness and anguish. However, now that they were given the prestigious position of being the *Mishkan* bearers, they were able to emotionally handle the fact that their count was so low.

The *sefer Matzdikei Harabbim K'kochavim* draws from this the message that the same psychological ploy must be utilized by *mechanchim* — and perhaps most when it is necessary to admonish a student. First build him up by pointing out his virtues. Only then proceed — cautiously — with the words of rebuke for the indiscretion (such as having asked a "*klotz kasheh*").

Had the rebbi of my childhood responded with, "Klein, that's an interesting question: let's talk about it at recess," or, "Klein, I am glad that you're finally asking *kushios* on the Gemara; let's discuss your question later," my childhood experience would have ended up as a constructive one instead of what it in fact was. One thing is certain: true humility was not engendered that morning.

(Perhaps this is a good spot to insert a plaintive plea to my fellow educators: avoid calling your *talmidim* by their last names. Doing so fails to endear you to them, and it inserts a useless gap between you and them. More than that, though, the love that a *melamed* is encouraged to feel for his *talmid*, being that it's supposed to be quasi-parental, precludes calling him by his last name. A parent not only calls his child by his first name; he might also add an endearing twist — such as Chaim'l, Sara'le, Yanki, etc. A *talmid* need be no different.)

After having considered several things to avoid in the bid to foster genuine humility in *talmidim*, let us turn to the correct methods for imparting it. But perhaps we need to first consider what this elusive character trait is to begin with.

In *Shemoneh Perakim* (ch. 4) the Rambam writes that *anavah* — ideal humility — is actually the median point between two negative extremes, one being *gaavah* and the other being *shiflus*, low-spiritedness. *Anavah* is as far from *shiflus* as it is from *gaavah*. Both extremes indicate, similar to what was noted above, that an individual's attentions are directed to himself. Proper humility consists of one's not viewing himself as different from others — neither for better nor for worse.

Consider this example: Years ago a certain Rav gave a weekly *shiur* which was nicely attended at first. After a while, despite that the *shiur* was excellent in both content and delivery, the attendance dropped significantly, to the point where the *maggid shiur* decided that he would stop saying the *shiur*. However, he was uncomfortable with how his decision would be viewed; so he told me, "I hope the *oilam* understands me. I'm not looking for *kavod*, but I'm also not looking for *bushos* (embarrassment)." I felt that there was great wisdom in those words: his decision was not lacking in humility, for *anavah* is in no way the same as shame.

In *Divrei Sofrim* (sec. 28) Reb Tzadok Hakohein of Lublin writes that true humility — or any ideal trait — is not something with which the individual is born, not something essential to his psyche. Rather it needs to be developed according to the principles of Torah and through a complete acceptance of Hashem's supremacy in all matters. Even Moshe Rabbeinu, he writes, the "*anav mikol adam*," the humblest of men, displayed signs of arrogance when doing so served the agenda of loyalty to Hashem. The focus of attention in the humble individual's mind is Hashem — not himself. That is true humility.

That makes the task of inculcating *anavah* in the hearts of *talmidim* a relatively simple one. Teach the child about Hashem at every turn. Relentlessly reinforce the thought that Hashem is the Source of everything — including the gifts of wisdom and intelligence with which individuals are blessed. As the child grows and as his awareness of the *Ribbono shel Olam* intensifies with time, his preoccupation with himself will decrease in turn — and not at the expense of his dignity and self-esteem.

GETTING TO KNOW ZUSHE!
THE ROLE OF *MESORAH* IN THE UPBRINGING OF CHILDREN

QUESTION: *My oldest son's tefillin have parshiyos with ksav Beis Yosef. My own are ksav Arizal. As I approach my second son's bar mitzvah and am about to order his tefillin, I feel that I may have done the wrong thing the first time around. I am leaning towards ordering Arizal, as that is the family's custom. This got me wondering: how important is the matter of mesorah to the upbringing of a child?*

ANSWER: At the outset, the halachic issue regarding which ksav is preferred lies beyond the parameters of this essay. Certainly both styles are based upon centuries-old mesorahs, and it is customary for each individual to practice his mesorah (pardon the redundancy!). If your minhag is indeed ksav Ari, then you probably should follow that. Your question, however, does not focus on tefillin per se, as much as it does on the general topic of the importance of mesorah in chinuch habanim.

It is important to note that the changing of a personal practice is a possibility. Though I have not checked the actual *teshuvah*, it is said that Rav Moshe Feinstein, *zt"l*, told an individual that the change from davening *nusach Sefard* to *nusach Ashkenaz* would be permissible.

My own personal experience rendered a similar conclusion. When many years ago I felt that I would like to change the *kesher* (and the style of putting on) *tefillin* from *Sefard* to *Ashkenaz*, I first asked my father, *z"l*, who had purchased my *tefillin* according to the Galicianer custom, that is, *Sefard*, if this would bother him at all. When he said it would not, I consulted with Rav Yitzchak Flakser, Rosh Yeshivah of Yeshivah Sfas Emes in Yerushalayim, to see if there might be a problem from the standpoint of halachah. He cited a related *psak* by the Kotzker Rebbe, as cited in *Siach Sarfei Kodesh*. That response was that the clause, "*Zeh Keili v'anveihu*" precedes "*Elokei avi va'aromemenhu*" in the *Shirah*. The clear message was that if an individual feels the need — for the sake of improvement in his own Yiddishkeit — to change an aspect of his *masores avos*, then he is permitted to do so.

Consider this related thought: I have noted on countless occasions that one of the greatest dilemmas for prospective *baalei teshuvah*, when they are about to actually commit to *mitzvos*, is that, in light of the diversity of various *mesorahs*, they do not know which set of practices to follow. There are *rabbanim* who have suggested to *baalei teshuvah* that they can simply choose the *mesorah* that provides for them the most spiritual fulfillment. This opinion clearly concurs with the aforementioned guidance. Interestingly enough, that approach has often resulted in "choices" being made that coincide with the *nusach* or the *minhagim* of the primary venue in which the particular *baal teshuvah* may have become *frum*.

For some people there will be difficulty in making such a decision: how exactly is one to know which set of *minhagim* appeals to one's *neshamah* most? Besides, the approach may lack personal appeal.

When I have been asked what to do by such individuals, I have on occasion suggested that they try investigating their own family history to attempt to determine what "brand" of Yiddishkeit their families subscribed to a couple of generations earlier, when they were Torah observant: in which town in Europe did they live, for example, which Chassidic court, if any, which yeshivah, and so on. And I posed the idea that it would be legitimate for them to pursue their own personal *mesorah*.

I discovered that this suggestion in fact provided much more than a solution to the practical dilemma of what to do: it actually also triggered a measure of excitement, which only increased as the investigations got under way. It provided for the individual a sense of somehow reconnecting with himself!

HEED THE TEACHING OF YOUR FATHER

An additional aspect emerges. One of the most famous statements pertaining to *chinuch habanim* is the *pasuk*, "*Shema beni mussar avicha…*" enjoining the son to heed the guidance of his father. That *pasuk* is cited by the *Baal HaMa'or* in a halachic context. The Gemara *Pesachim* (52a) states that the question of whether one may work on *erev Pesach* is determined by the custom of one's hometown. As to why that is important, the *Baal HaMa'or* posits that a legacy from home is part and parcel of what was meant by Shlomo HaMelech in his statement of "*Shema beni*." That is the ultimate fulfillment of the *chinuch* enterprise.

A SENSE OF IDENTITY

Every individual has an underlying need for a sense of identity, and one of the colossal *nisyonos* any individual might have is when he sees himself — or that he feels that others perceive him — as nothing more than non-crucial parts of an indistinguishable mass of reality. Whatever can be done to provide one with a specific sense of self is beneficial to one's self-concept and his self-worth, both of which, in moderation, are key components to one's capacity for growth.

That is true on a specific personal and psycho-emotional plane, but it is also relevant to the collective plane, which is the one on which the issue of *mesorah* appears. Consider the words of *Midrash Rabbah* (*Devarim* 16) regarding the flags that uniquely identified each of the twelve *shevatim* in the *Midbar*. "When Yisrael emerged from the sea, Hashem said to Moshe, 'Make them flags so that they will march with the ceremony of kings.'" The symbolism of the flag is the promotion of one's prominence. *Klal Yisrael* underwent their coronation on the basis of each *shevet* being given a specific flag to represent its regal essence.

And consider the *Yalkut Shimoni* (*Bamidbar* 2, *remez* 684). "A great love did Hashem express to Yisrael in that He made them 'flags' as the angels: this was in order that the sons of Reuven be recognized unto themselves and the sons of Shimon be recognized unto themselves." It was a manifestation of Divine love for each Jew to have the opportunity to identify himself as distinct, and as belonging to a specific group.

A STANDARD TO LIVE UP TO

One of the most famous Chassidic stories is that of Rebbe Zushe (of Anipol), *zy"a*. For years he lived in fear of one day going to the Heavenly court and being asked why he was not as great as his brother Rebbe Elimelech (of Lizhensk), *zy"a*. Then he dreamt one night that he in fact ascended to the *Beis Din shel Maalah* and was asked why he had not been as great as… Zushe! The *chinuch* message that emerges from that story is as often repeated as it is crucial. Do not live with the agenda of emulating someone else; merely try to live up to your own potential. Yet, as vital as this message is, it is predicated upon a basic principle: a person needs to have a self-image to begin with. How could Zushe be as good as Zushe if Zushe were not to know what or who Zushe is?

That idea is relevant not only to the quantity and quality of one's achievements; it pertains also to what course of action a person will choose to pursue. A child who knows that he is a member of a specific sub-community, with its own unique practices — from dress code to actual *minhagim*, from *nusach* of *tefillah* to the decision on which *poskim* to follow —is heir to much more than a legacy that is given to him. He becomes heir to a self-image as well, and that is crucial to his or her development. That self-image, assuming it is inculcated into the child with enthusiasm and love, is translated into a standard to which the child feels the need to live up.

That is crucial to a child's *chinuch*.

So while we cannot make the determination of which *ksav* is worthier from the standpoint of halachah, I would say that a *mesorah*, when it is presented as something to cherish, is an essential component in the overall effort of producing a generation of Yidden who are proud.

THE QUEST FOR REFINEMENT

QUESTION: *If it is true that derech eretz among our youth is deteriorating, what can be done to improve the situation?*

Pursuit of *middos tovos* among our children is a recurring theme. The question is rather apropos during the days of the *sefirah*, being that then we observe our annual partial mourning to commemorate the loss of R' Akiva's disciples. They died in an epidemic orchestrated by Hashem as punishment for that very flaw — a shortcoming in the area of interpersonal skills.

What is often asked, however, is that the *yemei hasefirah* were initially designated as exclusively joyous, as we excitedly count from the celebration of *Yetzias Mitzrayim* — the first component of our national freedom — to the monumental climax of *kabbalas haTorah*, the culmination of that freedom. Why, then, were specifically such festive days chosen by the Creator to "host" the horrific epidemic that felled thousands of great Torah scholars?

A common view is that the choice was deliberate because of a crucial lesson that is derived. As we prepare for the gift of Torah, we must recognize that without the groundwork of *derech eretz* and *kavod chaveirim*, there cannot be a proper *kabbalas haTorah*. Torah itself must sit upon a strong foundation of *menschlichkeit*. If it does not, it cannot be sustained with stability in the Jewish mind.

That *mussar haskel* is an essential lesson to be inculcated in today's yeshivah students. As they aspire to academic excellence, as they all set their aims on becoming the "best boy in the yeshivah," they might lose sight of the famed dictum of *Chazal* that *derech eretz* "*kadmah*" — precedes — Torah, and they consequently pay too little attention to the set of priorities that emerge from it.

With that articulated, it is worth noting that the question concerning how we might better educate our youth in the acquisition of *middos tovos* is a perennial one. One important addendum, though, needs to be stated. The question is asked with a greater sense of alarm today than it used to be in the past. The quest for *middos tovos* becomes more urgent with the passage of time. This has created a pressing educational need to address the issue.

To be sure, there are organizations — among them, one famous group located in Toronto, with another notable foundation based in Monsey — that have accepted the pedagogic challenge. For years they have labored furiously at offering schools programming and guidance in the development of teaching strategies. Creating and using an impressive array of media devices, reading materials, lesson plans, contests, and interactive experiences for children, they are helping the world of *chinuch* deal with the highly complex issue of *middos*.

At the same time, as noted, the times in which we live have added complications of their own, making the agenda of even the finest *derech eretz* program harder to realize, and making the goal of producing refined children even more difficult to achieve. Let us consider a number of these complications.

The "infiltration" of technology. With an increasing number of cellular phones, computers, answering machines, and emailing, people are lacking occasions in which to connect with others. It is harder to learn interpersonal skills today, in our society that increasingly limits people's need to interact with one another. Children require so-called "hands-on experience" in real people situations in order to be taught what makes certain responses socially and *hashkafically* acceptable while others are not.

Inequitable distribution! Though we cannot and would not espouse the forced implementation of a financially classless society, we recognize that there are tests inherent in wealth. It is as the *pasuk* says, "*Pen esba v'kichashti* — lest I become satiated and deny Hashem." The tests that go hand in hand with the growth of Jewish wealth are the possible promulgation of arrogance and a heightening sense of entitlement among us. These mindsets are variations of "*v'kichashti*," for they go contrary to truly "G-dly" behavioral standards. Prosperity will thus weigh heavily on our ability to refine the characters of our children. In a word, less refined parents will not likely produce more refined progeny.

Stress levels. More is expected of us today than in any period in recent memory. Our work hours are long; our output, being that we are assisted by such "helpful" hi-tech hardware, is expected to be higher. This generates aggravated stress levels in individuals. Most of our womenfolk have entered the work force, a factor that measurably restricts mothers' wherewithal needed for mothering. They, too, are under pressure, a mood they pass on to their families. This pressure that defines so much of modern life does not only hold us back from active parenting, but worse: it also transforms parents into poorer role models.

This last point is eminently worthy of our concentration, for there is no tool that is more effective than role modeling.

Consider the following paraphrasing of the words of the Slonimer Rebbe, in *Nesivei Chinuch* (ch. 3): In all education, the teacher's personification of what he is teaching is vital. However, his being a role model is limited to the areas in which his students are exposed to his influence. When it comes to educating the *penimiyus*, the inner character of a Jewish child, the importance of the positive role model and his influence on the child also reach the realm of the *penimiyus* of the educator. Jewish children are *bnei nevi'im*, scions of a legacy of prophecy. Accordingly, they are blessed with great astuteness and the ability to grasp the inner self of the *mechanech*. Therefore, if the *mechanech* teaches the child the importance of, say, self-control in dealing with physical desires, or of tolerance, compromise, and avoidance of anger and haughtiness in dealings with others, then children will absorb these values. If, however, the *mechanech* himself — in his personal life — does not portray accordance to these values, then the preachment becomes uselessly synthetic.

We do stand a reasonable chance of cultivating *derech eretz* in our children. This can and will occur if and only if the child perceives that *derech eretz* is a priority to the adults who comprise the role-modeling world that shapes the child. And the Slonimer Rebbe was undoubtedly referring to all the *mechanchim* in the child's life.

Now, while it is obvious that a *mechanech* — that is, in the conventional sense — needs to exhibit the highest standards of *derech eretz*, it is also of paramount importance that parents recognize their own role, one that is even more crucial. Consider that when a child is praised as being refined, or a *"baal derech eretz,"* the people who feel most entitled to feeling proud are his parents — not his rebbi. This is because of a *prima facie* link between their own role modeling and between their child's character. The corollary to that sense of pride, then, is the immense parental responsibility to ensure that they personify only the best traits of character.

Indeed, today's adult is perhaps compelled to deal with a plethora of complexities the likes of which his predecessors never even dreamed. However, most compelling of these is the educational imperative of being exemplars of character refinements that are in keeping with the *ratzon Hashem*. Only that will advance our hope of turning out children who will be the same.

SECULAR... BUT NOT SECULARISM — PART ONE

QUESTION: *How do secular studies fit into the chinuch equation?*

Right at the outset, let it be stated that this "whether-or-whether-not" question is for *Gedolei haTorah*. "*Talmideihem anu u'mipihem anu chayin*"; life's greater issues are determined by them. A number of pronouncements — though not necessarily uniform — have already been made concerning *limudei chol*. Directives from *Gedolei Eretz Yisrael* often differ from those in America, as locale has bearing on the matter. So, each *mosad* — indeed, each individual — needs to follow the specific *hadrachah* provided by its (or his) *moreh derech*. All we can do within this context, then, is discuss the issue, exposing some of what lies at its crux.

TYPES OF STUDY

First it is important to distinguish between types of secular academic pursuits. Some subjects are learned in order to provide what is called *"cognitive perspective"* to students. For instance, students are often exposed to varied literature, because it provides this nebulous cognition, while not being crucial to their futures.

It can be argued that such study jeopardizes strong Jewish sentiments in youth, although it has frequently been seen to enhance their minds. The Gemara (*Sotah*) declares a curse upon one who immerses himself or his child in *"chochmah Yevanis,"* teachings foreign to Torah. Accordingly, Torah schools need to carefully scrutinize all curricular choices.

Conversely, even within this broad category of study, there is knowledge that harmlessly gives students a healthy familiarity with the world. While many would suggest that the study of Shakespeare, for example, can be avoided, is there danger in studying geography or history (especially as these can impact on Jewish affairs)?

Other secular learning is skill-oriented (not content-oriented), providing practical tools to help students later. Such pursuits are meritorious, though language skills and basic math are understandably more worthwhile than trigonometry and physics, for most people. This category of study, though lacking the intrinsic value that Torah has, has extrinsic value, serving real objectives.

Therefore it is vital, even before the "discussion" commences, that its parameters be established. Should yeshivah students study English? Well, if that means the poetry of Lord Byron, perhaps not; but if it means communicative linguistic skills, such as rules of grammar and composition, then perhaps yes. For the sake of this discussion, let's speak about studies that have extrinsic value in our lives.

BITUL TORAH

One issue is *bitul Torah*, failure to spend time properly in Torah study. How could one have *talmidim* spend precious time studying math and grammar when they should be devoted entirely to Torah study?

A number of points are crucial. First, needless to say, *bitul Torah* is less problematic with *chinuch habanos* than *chinuch habanim*. As girls do not have the same imperative of *talmud Torah* as their brothers, there is less difficulty in their studying other things. *Bitul zman* — wasting time in general — is equally undesirable in girls and boys; but if a girl pursues secular learning, neither *bitul Torah* nor *bitul zman* occur (although there may possibly be damaging influences, depending on what she studies).

Secondly, we are given explicit instructions by *Chazal* to teach our sons practical livelihood skills. Although life spent fully in Torah study is the higher ideal, it must be false that pursuing livelihood skills involves *bitul Torah*. So, where secular study is concerned, if it has extrinsic merit, it is not *bitul Torah*.

A third factor is connected to the second. The late Telshe Rosh Yeshivah, Rav Mordechai Gifter, often said that when a *bachur* fails to apply himself to English, the problem extends beyond his not doing well in English: it is also *bitul Torah*. The reasoning is elementary: since one is obligated to study Torah always, the only other things he may do are necessary or worthwhile things. That is the *"heter"* to learn English. But if one abuses the time allotted to secular learning, why is he not learning Torah? That is when *bitul Torah* occurs.

LANGUAGE STUDY

There are two factors that ought to cause one to wonder about the significance of studying at least some measure of *limudei chol* — specifically language and communicative skills.

First, (pardon my presumptuousness) if the reader comprehends the ideas written here, it is because someone was taught writing skills (in some measure!).

Yet, for that, it might suffice for only *some* to have secular knowledge, without it impinging upon the curriculum of others. This reminds one of the encounter between Sir Moses Montefiore, the British Jewish philanthropist and the Chiddushei HaRim, *zy"a*. The former argued that Mordechai's understanding of foreign languages enabled him to understand the conspiracy of Bigsan and Seresh; this ultimately led to Jewish salvation. We might therefore conclude, he said, that it was the norm among our forbears to engage in secular learning.

To this the Chiddushei HaRim countered that in fact we deduce the opposite. If it would have been common for Jews to study languages, this would have been known, and the two conspirators would have refrained from discussing their plot within earshot of Mordechai. It was because they knew that Jews did not pursue foreign languages that they conversed openly.

Why, then, did Mordechai in fact understand Tursis? As is well known, it was required of all members of Sanhedrin to comprehend live testimony delivered in any of the classical seventy languages, with no intercession of interpreters. Thus Mordechai knew Tursis.

The only conclusion, though, that can be drawn is that it is sufficient for "some" Jews to be conversant in foreign languages and their associated cultures. No case for a pervasive undertaking of secular learning can be made.

The second concept, however, is more compelling — at least at first glance.

There have been numerous famous instances of how we have championed other languages — for noble purposes, such as combating negative influences.

When the Kara'im darkened the spiritual skies over *Klal Yisrael* in the ninth century (C.E.) their successes were attributable to their intellectual acumen and command of linguistics. The best way of engaging them in religious battle was to outdo them at their game. That is what R' Saadia Gaon did. In producing his dictionary of *Lashon HaKodesh* as well as his translation of Tanach into Arabic — not to mention his monumental Arabic classic, *Emunos*

VaDeios — he single-handedly won back the hearts of masses of Jews. That approach would have been unavailable had R' Saadia possessed no linguistic excellence — in Arabic as well as *Lashon HaKodesh*.

The Rambam used Arabic similarly, impacting upon the failing *emunah* widespread in his day. The *Igros HaRambam*, written in Arabic, saved thousands of Yidden from leaving Torah in pursuit of, *l'havdil*, other faiths.

More recently, the Germanic eloquence of Rav Shimshon Rephael Hirsch was instrumental in offsetting the possible impact of such works as Mendelssohn's *Bi'ur*.

Indeed, when the Imrei Emes, along with other *Gedolim* in pre-Holocaust Europe, encouraged the establishment of *Torah-dige* Yiddish journalism, it was to counter the inroads made by the secular Jewish press. The caliber of writing in the *frum* "*Yiddishe Togblatt*" had to reflect linguistic skill if it would stand the scrutiny of comparison.

Illustrations abound proving the need for at least some of *Klal Yisrael* to develop communicative know-how. That means some measure of secular language study.

SECULAR... BUT NOT SECULARISM — PART TWO

REGIONALISM?

After having previously discussed some of what is at stake in the issue of *limudei chol*, and after having distinguished between content-oriented and skill-oriented studies (with the former being declared much more problematic), we still found ourselves in a philosophical quagmire. So, as to whether *limudei chol* ought to be taught in our yeshivos, it is genuinely difficult to suggest a single, definitive, and a universally accepted stance on the topic.

It cannot be overly reiterated that the wisdom providing prescriptive statements on the issue must come from *Gedolei Torah*. We have seen, though, that there appears to be, even within *daas Torah* some regionalism in pronouncements. That is not to be construed as a sign of our times, for we have witnessed the like in past epochs too. For example, just as Rav Shimshon Rephael Hirsch stated the directive of *Torah im Derech Eretz*, stressing the need for secular study in Germany, so did the directives of the Chafetz Chaim and the Gerrer Rebbe oppose it in Lithuania and Poland.

Let us consider, however, that ideal called "*Torah im Derech Eretz*," for it does seem to entail a *shitah*, a clear policy that in a preferred state of educational affairs, a regimen of secular learning by Torah students will be included. Personally, I have heard varying interpretations of the ideal. Some hold that this policy is applicable in all situations and times, as per what *Chazal* taught in *Avos*. It is, in their view, "*l'chatchilah*."

Others, on the other hand, feel that Rav Hirsch merely designed an educational policy suited to the needs and conditions of his own sphere of influence. The Jews of Germany during the nineteenth century were strongly attracted by the spirit of what was perceived as and labeled "emancipation." Consequently, Rav Hirsch would likely have decided that if a Torah life would preclude all measure of secular learning, the consequence would be that an increasing number of Yidden would forsake their Torah lifestyle. (As it happened, untold religious damage in fact occurred there because of the *Haskalah*.) They would argue that in the lands to the east, where — at least for the while — the pull of so-called "liberation" was not nearly as strong, Rav Hirsch would surely have posited that secular studies are not to be included in the learning regimen of Torah students, as indeed the *Gedolim* in Poland ruled.

Furthermore, even if the dispute over how to interpret the teachings of Rav Hirsch were resolved, an equally pressing question would need addressing: how does one categorize contemporary Jewish society in North America? Might it be the cultural equivalent of nineteenth-century Germany? Or do we live in what would be more likened unto nineteenth- (and even twentieth-) century Poland, Lithuania, and Hungary, where *limudei chol* were not acknowledged as necessary? Is there a Jewish societal urgency that will be lessened if secular studies are included in yeshivah curricula?

UNIVERSALITY?

In the *Imrei Daas* of Rav Michel Yehudah Lefkovitch, we find a plaintive cry that ultimately nothing should be added to Torah study. Citing the second *pasuk* in *Tehillim*, "*Ki im b'Toras Hashem cheftzo,*" meaning that "*ashrei ha'ish,*" fortunate is the person whose pursuit is exclusively Torah, he argues against all pursuits that are, for all intents and purposes, extraneous to Torah. That is the meaning of "*ki im*" — exclusivity. David HaMelech was indicating a precise and exclusionary agenda: Torah and nothing else! Based on this, then, how could any yeshivah proceed to structure its academic program to include anything that is not Torah?

That sentiment speaks to a universal and not regionalist point of view. Indeed, other *Gedolei Yisrael* in the Holy Land issued similar statements in the past. And although there are those who suggest that the intent was always to be directed at Israeli yeshivos only, a *pasuk* in *Tehillim* speaks to universality.

Indeed, at a recent Torah Umesorah convention, one prominent U.S. Rosh Yeshivah declared — and to a North American audience! — that the yeshivah system of North America would never produce as much of the same level of excellence in Torah as what is achieved in Eretz Yisrael today, and that, he said, is because the traditional yeshivah system in Eretz Yisrael has no secular studies at all. And notwithstanding the fact that a number of other Rashei Yeshivah took slight issue with his position, even they, who seemed to feel that secular learning can be allowed here, agreed that it is merely a necessity of our times. That, needless to say, falls short from being a categorical statement of its being an essential ideal. Jewish ideals should be universal.

Another indication of universalism, though interestingly and ironically pointing toward an opposite directive, was evidenced from an experience I once had with a prominent Chassidishe Rosh Yeshivah from Eretz Yisrael, visiting in this country. He averred, and rather vehemently at that, that a problem within the yeshivah system of Eretz Yisrael today is that it provides no worldly skills to its students. It is a source of embarrassment, he said, that even for the most fundamental literacy skills, such as completing basic government forms and performing simple banking activities, *yungeleit* commonly need to rely on the skills of their wives, because they have none of their own. This is a proverbial black eye on the overall profile of today's yeshivah product, he stated.

This might be a good spot to interject a word of apology of sorts. One normally expects to read words that address a specific topic and to come away from the read with a definite sense of what constitutes the correct approach. This current piece, even as the earlier of its two parts was, fails to be conclusive — but only because the guidance that is forthcoming is anything but conclusive. Yet, despite that, there are a number of universal imperatives (or, at the least, observations) that can be offered on the subject. These I share.

There appears to be little harm done when *bnei Torah* and *bnei aliyah*, true Torah scholars, and righteous Jews, in addition to pursuing Torah knowledge with excellence, also achieve the ability to express themselves intelligently and perform elementary mathematical calculations.

Each Jewish locale needs to cater to its local needs and assumptions. Circumstances vary, as do mindsets, needs, and expectations. These can make a difference. And besides, there seems to be a sense of *regionalism* in *daas Torah* on this topic to begin with.

For the sake of outreach, it is an imperative (though arguably not upon everyone!) that Torah scholars be sufficiently erudite to communicate with those Jews who are as yet non-initiated in the faith and ways of their people. This requires more than a minimal level of verbal skill. If there can be no intelligent conversation among segments of our people, the gap between them widens, *Rachmana litzlan*.

In schools that do have a secular studies program, if students fail to apply themselves to it with due seriousness, they are guilty of *bitul Torah* — and not "*bitul chol*."

In some instances of yeshivos that have secular learning, it is common that children — or adolescents — make a mockery of the enterprise. This can begin with a disregard for what is being taught, and it can end with the actual victimization of English teachers and *chillul Shem Shamayim*. If a yeshivah cannot ensure decorum, and inadvertently allows *talmidim* to acquire rudeness and other negative character traits, it is better for the secular program to be scrapped. If *derech eretz kadmah laTorah*, if good behavior precedes Torah study, then it surely precedes secular study.

The concept of which we are required to be wary is secularism, for that is what threatens our adherence to Torah. Curriculum must be carefully examined so as to avoid even the slightest promotion of secularist values.

Even if secular studies can be a necessary evil, it surely need not be viewed as necessarily evil.

The real enemy is not that which is secular: it is that which is secularist. Secularism is undoubtedly an unnecessary evil, but what's worse, it is necessarily evil.

"COMMENCEMENT" EXERCISES

QUESTION: *What is the most central concept in formulating an ideal and all-encompassing approach for the chinuch of our children?*

There are so many pivotal components of the *chinuch* puzzle that it is practically impossible to isolate a single aspect and label it as the most central. That being said, however, to open the discussion, it is worthwhile focusing on the basic definition of *chinuch*.

When one inspects the instances of the verb *ch'n'ch'* in Tanach, it almost invariably denotes beginning: "Chanukas haMishkan," "*Mi ha'ish asher banah bayis v'lo chanacho*," and more. They all refer to the start of a process. In fact, Rashi clearly states in *Parashas Shoftim*, "*Chanoch, lashon haschalah*," that the word is translated as commencement.

Now, the definition of "beginning" entails that there be a continuation. And even if the process has no end, the process itself is necessary, if the use of the word "beginning" is to be valid at all.

The upshot is this: the fundamental motif surrounding *chinuch* is that there is a perceived process ahead — a goal or a sense of direction. I would suggest that all activity must somehow serve the pursuit of that goal.

CHINUCH BEGINS A PROCESS

On one level, that can be expressed as a sprawling philosophical macro-concept, a designation of the ultimate purpose of Jewish education in general: such that it furnishes a pervasive sense of self in the mind of a Yid. But while that is a very crucial thought in its own right, even more crucial to this context is how, on another level, this idea of beginning a process needs application, as a micro-concept, on a simple, everyday plane.

A thought that dwells universally in the minds of productive people everywhere is that there is a purpose to the day, the week and so on. Almost as soon as he wakens in the morning, the industrious person thinks about what he needs to achieve that day. In spiritual matters the very same holds true. First, as a macro-concept, consider what is taught in the very first *perek* of *Mesillas Yesharim*: it's most crucial for a person to clarify what is his purpose in existence in this world. The notion that one needs to accomplish something is a precondition to growth.

Yet, there are situations in which the prospects of the upcoming day's activities create negativity in one's mind — so much so that even when measurable achievements are made by the individual, the achievements might be completely devoid of significance and offer no gratification. This syndrome became prevalent as a result of the Industrial Revolution and the advent of the manufacturer's assembly line. The individual who turns the same crank over and over again, or fastens the same bolt thousands of times during the course of the day, becomes so alienated from the labor of his own hands and so disgusted by his routine that the only possible gratification he derives from his activity is the paycheck. He does not see the ultimate construction of a car as his *tachlis*, because it is neither *his* car nor *his* accomplishment — as he is tied to his mini-activity. When such a worker rises from sleep in the morning, he will predictably feel no excitement, no enthusiasm, no sense of purpose in what he envisions will be his work day.

(Indeed, though it may be nothing more than an urban myth, word has it that the "Monday car," built in the automobile assembly plant on a Monday, is liable to be plagued by poor workmanship due to the nihilistic sense of despair felt by assembly workers at the beginning of what will surely be a meaningless week at work.)

In *Parashas Vayeishev*, when Yosef HaTzaddik is instructed by his father to go inquire after the welfare of his brothers, he goes on his way and encounters a man who, Rashi explains, is Gavriel HaMalach. The "man" asks Yosef, "*Mah tevakesh* — what do you seek?" to which Yosef responds that he seeks his brothers. The Kotzker Rebbe explains that the message in that encounter — especially in light of the fact that Yosef's encounter was with an angel of Hashem, was symbolic and vital. When a person proceeds along his way, he must bear in mind that he needs to seek something. Goals are crucial. Goals imply direction and process.

There is no doubt in my mind that, insofar as this is a basic feature of the human condition, it will apply to all people — including children as they grow. A child who in the morning draws no enthusiasm from the prospects of what awaits him, sees school as purposeless drudgery. He has no sense of goal. This plays against his *chinuch*.

What comprises good *chinuch*, however, is the child's developing specific objectives in his learning. To instill a sense of eagerness — "*cheishek*" — for Torah in a child, it is important that the child be provided with goals in learning. Arguably, though, very few children will be motivated by the macro-concept —

the importance of developing into a Torah scholar and a devout Jew: those objectives are both too esoteric and too distant for a growing child to keep in his crosshairs. However, smaller, attainable and meaningful goals can be set for a child so that he will experience that fundamental human drive at the beginning of his day.

In one of the schools I had occasion to visit, I noted that its primary-grade *talmidim* were learning eagerly. They were doing worksheets, reviewing and testing one another, despite that there was no rebbi around prompting them, no test planned for which they were preparing, no class decorum they were attempting to honor. In fact it was their recess! Yet all of the children were involved voluntarily in their learning. That sounds like a simple statement, but it is anything but simple, usually reserved as a special compliment used in the report cards of better-than-average children.

When I commented to the *menahel* that the eagerness with which children were learning was remarkable, he revealed to me the educational tool that was responsible for the phenomenon. The children spend time both with teachers and with one another setting for themselves specific goals for their day. This goal setting is actually part of their school day. Very few motivators can parallel this for the potential to drive children.

Rav Yitzchak Hutner once cited the view of Rabbeinu Yonah to explain the well-known verse in *Mishlei* (27:21), "*V'ish l'fi mehallelo.*" The plain understanding of the *pasuk* is that one is defined on the basis of those who praise him, a trend to which we can all attest. Still, explained Rav Hutner, there is a more profound reality to which the words hint. "*Mehallelo*" needs not mean only "those who praise him." It can also mean "what he praises."

By definition, the achievements to which a person aspires are the things that are most praiseworthy for him. Train a child to set goals and aspirations for himself. He will be driven by the idea that he is in a process of growth — a journey that will lead him to great things.

IMPARTING AHAVAS ERETZ YISRAEL

According to *gedolei ha-mechanchim* of the contemporary era, one of the primary tasks to be performed by today's *rebbeim* and *morah*s is the instruction of their young charges in "*yesodos ha-emunah*," the fundamental tenets of our faith. Thus, educators are imparting the basics: the thirteen principles (*ikkarim*), the importance of *emunas chachamim*, *middos tovos*, and so on. I often wonder, though, what role, if any, Eretz Yisrael, as an ideal, currently plays within the mainstream of Torah *chinuch* in North America.

For starters, consider a number of elementary ideas:

Every time we recite *Birkas HaMazon*, we thank the Almighty for the "pleasant, good, and broad land" of our fathers, because the gist of the *mitzvah* is just that: to bless Him for the "good land that He has given you."

The Rambam tells us in *Hilchos Melachim* (5:10): "The greatest of our sages used to kiss the ground of Eretz Yisrael and roll about in its earth."

R' Yehudah HaLevi's lament "*Libi bamizrach, va'anochi b'sof hamaaravah* — My heart is in the east, while I am at the edge of the west," rings timelessly in the Jewish heart.

As we get into the *musaf* recited on any Yom Tov, we bemoan, "*U'mipnei chata'einu galinu me'artzeinu v'nisrachaknu me'al admaseinu* — And as a result of our sins we were banished and distanced from our land."

It certainly appears that the longing for Eretz Yisrael expressed by such often-mournful statements — only a small sampling of the many — should constitute a mighty force in the world of Jewish emotion. The love of the Land and the desire to live there ought to form a central theme for us.

Sadly, they do not. How ought we to deal with this discrepancy?

Far be it from me to declare a categorical imperative to move to Eretz Yisrael today. Our leaders have for many generations refrained from announcing such a directive; and illustrious *poskim*, such as the *Avnei Neizer, zt"l*, discussed at length the reasons that we are not necessarily obligated to make the move at this time. In fact, excluding the occasional exceptions, as a rule we choose to remain residents of *chutz la'aretz*. So, no brash statements shall be made here.

At the same time, although there does not seem to be a universal mitzvah to move to Eretz Yisrael (yet), I would argue that there is an absolute *mitzvah* to *love* Eretz Yisrael. The *Kli Yakar* explains (*Devarim* 1:6) that when Moshe cited Hashem's words to the people, "*Rav lachem sheves bahar hazeh* — You have dwelt at this mountain a long time," the intention was to rebuke the people for "hating the Land," that is, for failing to feel the love for Eretz Yisrael and enthusiasm about moving there. Indeed, he adds, that was Hashem's first *tochachah* to *Klal Yisrael* in the context of *Devarim*.

I often feel, though, that while genuine *ahavas Eretz Yisrael* is a Jewish ideal, it is sorely lacking in the equation of what fills young Jewish hearts today. We determinedly inculcate into our children and students an appreciation for *ahavas Hashem, ahavas haTorah*, and *ahavas Yisrael*; but *ahavas Eretz Yisrael*, on the other hand, has not been accorded a respectable spot in the educational agenda.

On numerous occasions I would ask *talmidim* how many had already had the opportunity to visit Eretz Yisrael. As time went by, the numbers of those who had would increase, probably the result of rising Jewish affluence and the increasing fashionableness of visiting the Land. And when I'd ask how many intended on studying there after secondary schooling years, more and more would raise their hands in the affirmative.

This is indeed the case, for eventually, when young yeshivah boys and Bais Yaakov girls come of age, they set their sights on Eretz Yisrael as the place to spend a year or two learning. And for many young *kollel* couples eager to keep up with the latest vogue, married life needs to commence in Eretz Yisrael, that is, until they are ready to "settle down."

With the additional fact that visiting Eretz Yisrael is extremely common among Western Jews today, it is valid to assert that the Holy Land is a real part of our lives. I wonder, though, what role it actually plays, for while it may be a temporary destination of choice, it is hardly an ideal.

Getting back to my classroom surveys, for example, when I would proceed to ask how many dreamt of one day moving to Eretz Yisrael, almost no one would answer yes. Apart from a scenario of the coming of Mashiach, living in Eretz Yisrael is just not a real goal. *Ahavas Eretz Yisrael* can therefore not be an ideal, for true love of the Land would manifest itself at least as a dream of living there. Thus, despite the fact that Eretz Yisrael is one of the components of how we Jews currently enjoy life, there is precious little genuine *ahavas Eretz Yisrael* being generated. This is arguably a fault in the planning of objectives in contemporary *chinuch*.

The question is how we ought to address it.

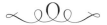

One of the calamities in this matter is the century-old distortion of the ideal itself in many a Jewish mind. As a result of the advent of secular — and even non-secular — nationalistic Jewish movements, the notion of loving the Land of Israel has been largely politicized. To some extent the original ideal has thus become hijacked, as it were, by those popular waves that can have no monopoly on *ahavas Eretz Yisrael*, but often pretend that they do. The ramification is such that references to love for Eretz Yisrael were almost deemed taboo among many observant Jews in *chutz la'aretz* during the past half-century. This was the consequence of their fear of being associated with a "Jewish" philosophy that sounds too similar to other "non-Jewish" nationalistic philosophies. Therefore, in yeshivos that cautiously distanced themselves from political alignment, the topic of *ahavas Eretz Yisrael* effectively was allowed to slip through the cracks.

Even the fact that countless *Gedolei u'Meorei haTorah* over the centuries professed their love of the Land could neither overpower nor contend with the new nervousness. The Baal Shem Tov, the Chasam Sofer, the Ohr HaChaim, *zecher tzaddikim livrachah*, and many others, not only wrote and spoke often of their yearning to be in Eretz Yisrael — they often actually took steps to make the move. Despite this, however, our own *mosdos* shied away from promoting this classical and traditional Jewish value, for fear of being labeled.

As far as the capacity that parents have to teach the ideal to their children, well, that has not been an easy task. In particular, one challenge to their promoting the ideal of yearning for Eretz Yisrael has prevented them from doing so — and with increasing potency. That challenge is prosperity. Yearning — for anything — is the handmaiden of privation. As a rule, only if one's current situation is lacking in some substantive way will one yearn for a different one. The obvious corollary is that if an individual is effectively content with his lot in life, he will not long for a change. And if one does not yearn, it is not likely that he will be able to instill yearning into his children.

The lifestyle that North American Jews presently enjoy lends itself more and more to the sensation that all is well. Not only is the material aspect of life predicated upon plenty and upon enjoyment, but we also have developed the notion that our spiritual lives are no less viable than they would be in Eretz Yisrael. We, *baruch Hashem*, have an ever-expanding range of Torah *mosdos*, shuls, *kollelim*, *shtiebelach*, and a rich assortment of "strictly kosher" consumerist amenities. In brief, a plethora of comfortable spiritual options! So what's there to yearn for?

True, we North American Jews clearly have much for which to be thankful. At the same time, there is one respect in which our Yiddishkeit — and therefore our *chinuch* — has been fundamentally compromised: it is our capacity for yearning. In the very first *siman* (*se'if* 3) of *Shulchan Aruch Orach Chaim*, we discover the link between privation and yearning. "It is fitting that everyone who fears Hashem shall be '*meitzar v'do'eig*,' grieve and be anxious, over the destruction of the Beis HaMikdash." While one can understand the role of grief, what is the role of this anxiety that every *yarei Shamayim* should experience? Furthermore, what is the link between grief and anxiety that they are mentioned in one breath?

The underlying concept, though, as noted earlier, is that there is a necessary link between the two. Grief is based upon, or perhaps synonymous with, the feeling of privation, for one grieves only for that which one no longer has. In like fashion we can say that anxiety is identical with yearning. What we derive from the words of the *Shulchan Aruch*, then, is that the two concepts are intertwined. So, it is exceedingly difficult for us to impart to our children a longing for Eretz Yisrael, if their sense of privation is limited to yet another pack of *Gedolim* cards or the most recently released music CD. Hence, the imperative of teaching our children to love and to yearn for Eretz Yisrael has been made difficult to achieve.

Difficult, perhaps, but not impossible!

Without depressing our *talmidim* and children about the fact that our present situation, as blessed as it often appears, is profoundly imperfect, we are well urged to *teach* them this essential lesson. Indeed, in the spirit of preserving a healthy equilibrium, we should rejoice over the democracy and prosperity that circumscribe our lives, on the one hand, but on the other, relentlessly internalize, first into ourselves and then into our young, the sense of privation in *galus* and the subsequent yearning for a better place and time. The theme ought to emerge during dinnertime conversation at home, as well as in the syllabus of Torah study at school.

In truth, just as pre-Pesach is the best time to teach the lessons of Egyptian bondage and our nation's deliverance, the most suitable time for strengthening *ahavas Eretz Yisrael* in our students is the "Three Weeks," during *Bein HaMetzarim*. However, save for a handful of locales around the world, schoolchildren are on vacation then. That fact, however, by no means absolves us from the sacred task of reconnecting the Jewish Land to the Jewish heart, according to the correct *ruach haTorah*.

May it be the will of Hashem that by the time the next *Bein*

HaMetzarim rolls along, we will no longer have to cultivate feelings of privation and yearning, and that we will be able to celebrate our *ahavas Eretz Yisrael* in the complete sense, *bevi'as hagoeil, Amein.*

PART TWO

יַסֵּר בִּנְךָ וִינִיחֶךָ וְיִתֵּן מַעֲדַנִּים לְנַפְשֶׁךָ

משלי כט:יז

PEDAGOGICAL PRACTICES
THAT BEAR MENTIONING

REACHING EACH AND EVERY ONE

QUESTION: *I am a rebbi in a large yeshivah. Our menahalim are eager for us to keep astride with many of the latest advancements in chinuch methodology so that we can always become better at what we do. One of the latest theories is called "Differentiated Instruction." What can you tell me about it?*

I will begin with three preliminary points. First of all, you really ought to consider yourself fortunate for being in a yeshivah that encourages its *mechanchim* to constantly seek self-improvement; that should be a more widespread goal — and in all fields.

Secondly, "Differentiated Instruction" is a pedagogic science that, like any other, has its experts whose guidance is available and should be sought; this column is not a venue for detailed professional development.

Thirdly, and I think quite importantly, "Differentiated Instruction" might indeed represent a fashionable turn of phrase denoting a number of fine, up-to-date, teaching recipes; however, as a concept, it has always been a feature of good pedagogy. It used to be referred to as "streaming" or simply as "individualization." It is also known as "grouping," whereby *talmidim* can be separated into smaller groups based on ability, on interest, on learning orientation, or even on a variety of aspects of their personal backgrounds.

The need is grounded in the fact that there might be essential diversity — something that a rebbi can analyze — pertaining to the way his students process, internalize, or retrieve information. Accordingly, there can and ought to be matching divergent instructional activities that the rebbe can use. And, there is little doubt about the need for, at the very least, diversity in the means of assessing and evaluating — and reporting — progress.

In truth, though, while some of the techniques may be fresh and new, the *hashkafah* itself is certainly not.

Consider the following: In *Darkei HaChaim* (pp. 174–175), Rav Michel Yehudah Lefkovitch discusses the issue that is classical yet current. In any class, he avers, there is a range of students, with some being talented, some of average ability and some who struggle. It can happen — and often does — that the rebbi is intellectually tempted by the idea of engaging the more talented *talmidim* and might proceed to discuss the learning with them at the expense of the others in the class.

While Rav Michel Yehudah does not suggest that the more advanced boys should not be taught at their advanced level, he does claim that it is a failing for an educator to ignore the needs of the rest of his *talmidim*. The rebbi "needs to devote thought regarding every *talmid*, concerning how to address him in an appropriate manner," he teaches.

He also shares a number of strategies for a rebbi to use in class. At the same time, *mechanchim* everywhere have contended with this challenge, and many have devised their own methodologies for dealing with it — on the practical level.

As a theory, however, "Differentiated Instruction," is, as noted, a universal *chinuch* imperative, and not a newfangled one. In *Nesivei Chinuch* (ch. 4, sec. 3) the Slonimer Rebbe writes, "The *mechanech* must recognize as a sacred obligation and as a top priority that general *chinuch* for all his charges is not adequate. Rather, one must provide individualized *chinuch* for each one, in accordance to his personality." So differentiation in instruction is quite a timeless Torah notion.

Although the concept of Torah's timelessness is deeply entrenched in every believing Jew, it profoundly excites the mind to come across that concept while discovering newness, finding a thought that is simultaneously contemporary and ancient — contemporary because it is discussed as if it were a fresh idea, and ancient because it emerges from a reading of our sacred texts.

This notion could well have unfolded recently if one would have stopped to ponder one of the classical lessons connected to the *arba'ah banim* mentioned in the Haggadah. Four sons, four distinct approaches — and all carried out ostensibly at the same time!

Now, while it is possible that the four sons ought not to be necessarily understood as actually being together at one venue, and while it is likely that the Haggadah is merely guiding fathers in how to deal with four distinct scenarios, it is also possible, as many of us indeed learned as children, that the four *banim* are in fact sitting together at the same *seder* table.

Each of the four has his own personality and inclinations, his own private agenda, mindset and even his own scripted lines (save for the *She'eino yodei'a lish'ol*). Yet, the father, who might have had difficulty enough handling any one of the four, is expected by the Torah — for after all the Torah itself speaks *k'neged*, or about, the four sons — to deal with all four, using four unique styles, one for each of his four sons. And the father is expected to juggle all the personalities and techniques at the very same time!

As a statement of imperative, though, the Haggadah's words are almost superfluous. In a fundamental way, the Haggadah need not convince the father about the need to reach each of his children, for every father naturally wishes to do so, and that, because his paternal love compels him to. It is only for sensing that many parents may lack the required skill to formulate responses to meet the divergent needs that the Haggadah assists them in structuring proper approaches for them. However, the need to answer each son *al pi darko,* according to his way, is an almost instinctive part of parenting.

The same certainly holds true for teaching.

Years ago I heard a *gadol b'Yisrael* offer a simple explanation of the words of *Chazal* (*Sanhedrin* 19b): "He who teaches Torah to another's child is deemed by the Torah to be as if he brought him into this world (*k'ilu yelado*)." More than a statement of reward or status for the Jewish educator, it is a statement of imperative, he declared. The statement of *Chazal* comes to urge the *mechanech* that his responsibilities are much the same as those of parents.

Fundamentally that seems to underscore the popular notion of "love," with the idea being that teachers need not merely display it, but need to actually feel love for the young charges with whom they have been entrusted. Certainly the concept of "loving one's *talmidim*" has been so bandied about in teacher training; still, that fact does not diminish its importance.

What is crucial, though, is that the statement of *Chazal* is not that the rebbi should make a "display" that will show *k'ilu yelado,* but rather to know that it is in fact the case. And differentiation is a vital component of this.

My experience in the field has shown me that all conscientious *rebbeim* and *morahs* do in fact entertain this unwritten agenda of wanting to reach every single child. The single most important issue that was brought before me in my "principaling" days was not discipline, but teachers having a hard time "reaching" specific students for whom the conventional teaching methods were just not working.

Indeed, if and when I ever experienced a personal sense of failure in *chinuch* from my many years in the classroom, it would have been only from such cases where a young person may have been in my personal pedagogical care for ten months and left almost un-impacted.

Every *mechanech* or *mechaneches* whose efforts are intended "*l'sheim Shamayim*" would be haunted by such a scenario. With that being the case, then the new popularity of the phrase, "Differentiated Instruction," merely helps to put the concern for individualization back to the position of front and center, where it belongs.

WE'VE LOST THE RIGHT

One of the most compelling issues in *chinuch* is the question of whether or not corporal punishment is to be used in the classroom.

The issue is reasonably complex to begin with — indeed pertaining to the classroom as well as to the home — but it has become much more complicated over the past few decades as a result of the altered views of society as a whole. And sometimes even our *shitos* are shaped by the attitudes and policies of the world around us. In Rav Shlomo Wolbe *zt"l*'s *Zriah U'Binyan*, for example, we find the thought that whereas children of long ago could tolerate physical means of punishment, today's cannot.

A pivotal point with which to begin analysis is the Torah's prohibition against striking another person in general. In the *para-*

shah of *malkus*, the Torah warns that the *shaliach beis din* may not add to the lashes he is to administer to the guilty party. When a lash that is not warranted by Torah law is given, he who has given it has transgressed the prohibition of *"lo yosif,"* he shall not add.

The same prohibition applies to any Jew who strikes another. But what about the initial thirty-nine lashes (or whatever amount the *beis din* assesses)? Why are those permitted? The obvious answer is that since the Torah has ordered that those lashes be given, they are a mitzvah, which means that they could not possibly be forbidden. The derived law, then, is that one may strike another if —and only if — it is a mitzvah for him to do so. The crucial question, then, would normally be this: when a *mechanech* hits a *talmid*, is he performing a mitzvah, or is he transgressing the prohibition of *"lo yosif"*?

Regarding this *Chazal* were clear: a *"rav ha'rodeh es talmido,"* a rebbi who hits his student, is doing a mitzvah. So much so, explains the Gemara in *Makos*, that even if the *talmid*'s behavior and learning are exemplary it is nevertheless beneficial to his development that he be hit (occasionally). The result is that a rebbi actually does a mitzvah by striking a *talmid*, regardless of the "deservingness" of the *talmid*.

The issue would therefore have seemed simple if not for the fact that hitting *talmidim* is widely frowned upon today. For example, a few years ago, the largest network of *chassidishe* schools in Eretz Yisrael (and possibly the world) received a directive from their Rebbe that corporal punishment is no longer to be used in the *chadarim*. The scenario by which *menahalim* are instructing their staffs to abstain from using *"petch"* is extremely common today. Rav Eliyahu Lopian was reported to have expressed regret for every time he hit any one of his eleven children. Rav Wolbe was quite emphatic in prohibiting the use of corporal punishment in *chinuch*.

So, in light of the words of *Chazal*, how do we formulate the correct understanding of this issue?

At a gathering of hundreds of *mechanchim* together with *Gedolei HaTorah*, one *gadol* expressed the view that whereas corporal punishment is the ideal tool of behavior modification in an ideal society, we in our own day "have lost the right to hit." When contemplating that statement, however, I wondered how it is possible for an apparent "ideal" to be reduced in such a manner, and for the right to exercise that ideal to be "lost."

Then it dawned upon me that there may in fact be a precedent for that idea. We find in Torah the mitzvah of *yibum*, whereby a man is obligated to wed the childless widow of his departed brother. This is for the express purpose of building a home and family "*al sheim achiv ha-meis*," so that the name of the dead brother shall not be erased. The alternative is the shameful option of *chalitzah*, whereby the brother is allowed to release his sister-in-law from the bond that links them, and whereby he is publicly disgraced for doing so.

The ideal situation in an ideal Jewish society is *yibum*. Yet, as the Gemara declares in *Kesuvos*, that option is no longer open to us, leaving *chalitzah* as the only choice. The reason, explain *Chazal*, is that we no longer are on the level of being able to do the mitzvah *l'sheim Shamayim*. *Yibum* is the sort of practice that must be done for the sake of the lofty goal of establishing progeny for the *niftar*. Otherwise it cannot be done at all! *Chalitzah* has therefore become the only choice.

That topic, then, serves as the possible precedent for the notion that it is possible for the Jewish people to have fallen spiritually and consequently to have lost the right to observe that which was actually the ideal in other circumstances and in other epochs. (Incidentally, as I write these lines, I am struck by ironic juxtaposition between *parashas makos* and *parashas yibum* in the very text of *Parashas Ki Teitzei*.)

What remains to be understood is the nature of our spiritual fall which has resulted in forfeiture of the ideal. In my estimation, there are two ingredients.

The first is that today's *talmidim* are not capable of handling physical rebuke. People tend to be more pampered and self-centered; children are, not surprisingly, more sensitive, with a stronger sense of entitlement. The best and softest *potch* is likely to be regarded as abusive in the eyes of today's children. Accordingly, it *is* abusive. We have been instructed by *daas Torah* to consider new realities and the changing times, for at times we must modify our technique based on the changes. That is one factor in the new *chinuch* wisdom.

A more compelling factor, however, puts the spiritual fall in the hands of the *mechanech* of today. In *Even Sheleimah*, the Vilna Gaon explains Shlomo HaMelech's enjoinder of *"chosech shivto sonei b'no* — he who spares the rod hates his son." The Gaon writes that a father who strikes his child must do so with no trace of anger. Even a parent who exercises the prerogative of *petch* must feel no anger as he does so. The intention that he must have is to educate and improve his child. The same, of course, would hold true for a rebbi who employs such methods with students. If the single *kavanah* that fills the rebbi's heart is the desire to benefit the child, then the ideal could have applied. Arguably, however, today's *mechanech* might fall somewhat short of the sublime spiritual place of the *mechanech* of long ago. Today's Jewish educator is perhaps more likely to be afflicted with the pressures and challenges of contemporary life, so that a move to hit a child could very well be venting his rage. And that, of course, is not the corporal punishment that would ever have been regarded by Torah as a pedagogic ideal. It is thus eminently comprehensible that the educators of today "have lost the right to hit."

TESTING…TESTING…1, 2, 3

One of the components believed to keep the wheels of *chinuch* turning is "testing." That which serves as an incentive for a student to be attentive and to review his or her material is the apprehension he or she might sense from the "testing-evaluating-reporting" process looming on the horizon.

In recent times, the Torah world, which has long incorporated some testing in the younger grades, has witnessed a slight increase in its use as a means of promoting learning. In many venues, however, testing still effectively stops at the post-secondary level, especially in the world of the *yeshivah gedolah*, where it is commonly felt that testing would insult the integrity of *talmidim*. Today, on the other hand, testing has gained wider acceptance, and there are often *bechinos* being administered even at the *kollel* level.

As far as the so-called insult to the integrity of older *talmidim*, it might be posited that if testing were to become the norm, it would cease to be an affront. In the secular world examinations are perfectly accepted at all levels of study. Even a doctoral candidate will be required to "defend a dissertation," which is just another form of being tested. Now, certainly the knowledge of Torah stands on a higher plateau than any secular study, and it needs to be "defended," so to speak, all the more. Therefore, there might be no legitimacy to the idea that a *bechinah* is a *pechisus hakavod*, or an insult.

Besides, the view that testing insults assumes that academic integrity in fact becomes properly galvanized among all *talmidim* as they get older. Certainly, there are individuals who do portray such sublime academic devotion, but they are the exceptions rather than the rule. The diversions of today's world make it harder for a student to "keep his nose to the grindstone"; so integrity has suffered. Besides, is it not obvious that integrity varies from person to person?

Additionally, as *Chazal* have taught, of every thousand *talmidim* who commence the journey of Torah study, only one reaches the ultimate goal. What happens to the rest? Might testing have helped them?

The answer is probably "yes": we need to encourage the use of tests. Our prime focus here, however, is not advocacy for testing itself, but rather the guidelines that ought to govern it. First and foremost, there needs to be concern on the part of educators that the aforementioned "apprehension" not be transformed into anxiety or fear. Those feelings in a student, if unbridled, can be emotionally destructive, and they will hamper learning instead of promoting it.

It is for this reason that three factors are worthy of mention as motifs for testing. A prelude to these, however, is the obvious but crucial postulate that we derive the basics of our *modus operandi* from Torah — in particular, for this context, from the Torah's description of Divine tests.

LET THEM SHINE

Why test students? Would schooling not be simplified if tests were not given? Would it not be easier for a teacher if there were no tests to grade? More fundamentally, though, doesn't the *mechanech* already know how his *talmidim* are doing without having to resort to actual *bechinos?* The answer is connected to why the *Ribbono shel Olam* tests us.

In *Parashas Re'eh* the Torah presents the scenario of a false prophet who has powers to perform miracles. If he is indeed a charlatan, one wonders why he was given such powers. The Torah explains that Hashem is merely testing the Jewish people in this manner. The Ibn Ezra comments: "*V'nisayon Hashem l'har'os tzidkas hamenuseh* — the tests of Hashem are given with the intention of exhibiting the piety of the one being tested." This view is shared by other commentators as well.

A test is to be given with the prime intention of providing an opportunity for the tested one to shine, to bring his potential to the state of the actual. The self-satisfaction that an adult gets from having done well on a test is akin to the feeling that a *mechanech* should want a student to feel as an outcome of a test. The student should end up radiating the happiness that comes from accomplishment. That should be the teacher's objective. Students will actually perceive this as the teacher's agenda; and they will respond accordingly.

TESTING KNOWLEDGE — NOT LACK OF IT

Related to that is the actual nature of tests.

In *Parashas Eikev*, we discover that Hashem's purpose in testing *Klal Yisrael* through the years in the *Midbar* was, "*Lada'as es asher bi'lvavcha*," to discover that which is in your heart. It was not to discover "*es asher ein bil'vavcha*," that which was not in your heart. Surely, considering that humans are imperfect, Hashem, when testing the nation, could simply have sought the gaps of faith and the shortcomings of commitment in *Bnei Yisrael*. But He did not!

Similarly, when we test *talmidim*, the orientation must be to discover the knowledge that they *have* acquired or mastered. It is not to reveal their academic failings, or the knowledge that they *have not* acquired. The nature of a test must be in accordance with this idea. As a result, questions should be simple and straightforward. And why would a teacher include "trick questions," if the goal is to help students display achievement? And yes, there is a legitimate place for the element of challenge within the realm of testing; however, the teacher should construct challenges in a way that will promote success. Modify quantities for students who need such modification. The ground rule is that students are not prey. Assist them in the goal of showing off their knowledge.

POSITIVE RESPONSES

Naturally, the achievements of students will vary. Indeed, a healthy sign in a class is that excellence is not too easy to attain. Consequently, a *mechanech* can easily expect incorrect answers occasionally. The manner in which a teacher will respond to these is of pivotal importance.

In *Parashas Kedoshim*, we are instructed to deal with the failings of others in the following way: "*Hocheiach tochiach… v'lo sisa alav cheit.*" Even if we need to admonish, we must admonish such that the sin does not devastate the sinner. When I bring a person's failing to the limelight, I must do so gently.

As a practicum for the teacher: do not mutilate the test with ugly red markings. Do not accentuate the errors by oversized Xs and "minus" designations. The student is most likely intelligent enough to discover what he did wrong if you point him in the right direction. There is thus no need to bang him over the proverbial head. A comment like "I'm sure you will do better next time," will help the student a lot more than pointless observations like, "Needs improvement," or, "What a disappointment!" (The student is disappointed enough without your bringing this to his attention.)

Any mechanism needs to be well-oiled and maintained to be operative. For the wheels of *chinuch* to be kept turning, so that motivated students are produced, testing — but specifically the desirable sort — will be beneficial indeed.

A LANGUAGE OF THE SOUL

When the semi-mournful days of the Omer arrive, many minds focus on the fact that we abstain from music. There are specific *halachos* governing this abstention, such as the *heter* for singing despite the prohibition against hearing instrumentals. In consideration of the fact that music is obviously seen as a contravention of the mood of *aveilus*, one might be curious as to why this is so. However, a specific *chinuch*-related question that arises from this focus concerns what role, if any, is played by music in *chinuch habanim*?

Indeed I was once asked by a group of *mechanchim* whether it was appropriate to use singing, or jingles, in class, to teach children to daven, to *bentsch* and so on. The questioners were concerned that the musical motif would diminish from the seriousness of the activity.

My response was that I was far more concerned that there appears to be a stream of consciousness among many *mechanchim* today that suggests that good *chinuch* needs to be infused with heaviness and a "no-smile" mood. I wonder what happened to the *Chazal* that teaches that the *Shechinah* resides among us exclusively within an atmosphere laden with *simchah* — and not *atzvus*, sadness. (See *Yerushalmi, Sukkah* 5:1.) Granted, *kalus rosh*, or light-headedness is never a vehicle for growth, but why connect music with *kalus rosh*? Were the *Leviim* in the Beis HaMikdash light-headed for being the songsters of our people in antiquity?

(It is important to interject at this point that this discussion is completely unrelated to some of the broader issues surrounding contemporary music — the modern rhythms, the question of concerts, the volume with which the band plays at weddings and so on. Those topics need to be determined by the sage counsel of *gedolim*. They are certainly not educational matters in the strict sense and therefore have no place in this context.)

Clearly, one must not get carried away with the use of music in the classroom — or anything else for that matter. A Yiddish idiom is "All that is 'too' is not good." Yet, just as an overabundance of certain nutrients is not beneficial, it remains true that a developing body does require a certain measure of almost all of them. The same can be argued for music within the emergence of a well-balanced and motivated learner. Let us consider some of the reasoning.

It is no secret that music possesses a soothing quality that can relax tensions. From the lullabies that a mother sings to her infant to the falsetto solos that adults often emit as they work and learn, the complex web of human emotions gets somewhat untangled when the strains of a melody fill our ears and hearts.

I shall never forget the sound of my late Rebbi, a brilliant Rosh Yeshivah, humming the *niggun* to "*Leiv tahor bera li Elokim*" as he was engrossed in thought attempting to unravel a *Tosfos*. And who is the man who spent time learning in yeshivos who does not recall the sounds of *bachurim* swaying to and fro over their Gemaras, singing while they learn as a means of discovering either inspiration or clarity?

It certainly stands to reason that an ambient melody could be helpful in any person's absorption of ideas, as long as it is ambient and not the primary focus. The same must therefore hold true of *talmidim* in a yeshivah setting. (The challenge, of course, is that for young people "background music" can easily grab their "foreground" attention, undermining the learning experience.)

It is said that the Baal HaTanya would often comment that "*negginah*" (that is, music with no words, as opposed to *zimrah*, music with lyrics) is the *kulmus*, the quill, of the *neshamah*. That suggests that the innermost and profoundest level of human consciousness expresses itself — both actively and passively — through the medium of music.

The reason that *chazanus* — liturgical music — as well as *niggunim* during davening are so prevalent is the same fundamental factor of the human condition: the pinnacle of *tefillah* is the soul's bid to connect with *HaKadosh Baruch Hu*, and nothing can serve as a more efficient conduit for that connection than the language of the soul. (It would be remiss to omit here the view of those, such as the *Mateh Ephraim*, who held that there ought perhaps not be singing during the *tefillos* of *Yamim Nora'im*, despite the fact that most *kehillos* do not practice this stringency — likely because of the aforementioned idea.)

In a similar vein, it is known that a renowned *gadol b'Yisrael* once commented that he might have been mistaken to have left the singing of *zemiros* out of the Shabbos-table experience when his own children were growing up, despite that it was replaced by learning.

One of the empirically verifiable truths about music is that it facilitates memory. Memory will be intensified by other concurrent activity that takes place in one's mind. That is why one will remember words that he has sounded out much better than words that he only reads silently. That explains the Mishnah's dictum regarding *Krias Shema*: "*Hashmi'a l'oznecha mah she'atah motzi mipicha*," hear that which you speak. It may also be a partial explanation for why one should ideally "*lein*" *Shema* with the *tropp*, the musical notations. We also recognize that media advertising that uses jingles makes a much stronger impact than that which relies only on text alone. It locks into one's memory and can be retained for a lifetime. (Of course, there is a negative idea that also emanates from that very fact.)

I know an excellent second grade *morah* who was able to instil into her students the names of the fifty-four *parshiyos* of the Torah in minutes — by simply using a different ditty for each *Chumash*. The names of those *parshiyos* stick in the minds of her *talmidos* permanently.

There is a relatively new — although in fact centuries-old — method of *chinuch habanim*, known as the Zilberman method. It is actually a contemporary application of the time-honored approach based on the teachings of both the Maharal and the Vilna Gaon, *zecher tzaddikim livrachah*. The system of teaching, which has regained much popularity in recent years, is geared towards infusing a wealth of knowledge into *talmidim* quickly, through copious review and through the wide use of chanting.

Any visitor to a "*Derech HaMaharal*" school — and they exist now in many large Jewish communities worldwide — will be struck by their command of the material and will be duly impressed by the joyous enthusiasm with which the boys learn. And undoubtedly one of the most significant components of their achievements in learning is the singing that accompanies the recitation.

That being said, children do need to be weaned from overabundant music in their learning and davening at an early age. However, the musical faculty can be used successfully for as long as children will react to it constructively, and they will almost inevitably revert to it later on again.

We find in *sifrei Chassidus* that the term *shirah* is etymologically connected to the word *yashar*, straight. The reason is that sublime and spiritual music in this earthly realm is parallel to the Divine song that is sung in *Shamayim*. So, as we prime ourselves for being somewhat distanced from Hashem via the removal of music during the grievous days of the *Sefirah*, we are also reassured that in the ultimate reality for which we pray (*Tehillim* 149:5), "*Ya'alzu chassidim b'chavod yeranenu al mishkevosam*," the song of joy will be inherently embedded into the consciousness of righteous people.

IGGUD: REMEMBERING INDIVIDUALS WITHIN THE GROUP
EXPLORING THE JOY INSPIRED WHEN WE TAKE THE FOUR MINIM ON SUKKOS

As his half-hour lunch break neared its end, Joe called his boss. "Mr. Smithers," he began. "Sir, I'm in a bit of a jam. I just found out that my wife's great-grandmother passed away this morning. Then, my wife called me to tell me that when she rushed to the hospital to see her — as she was trying to avoid that tornado we had — she had a terrible accident, and her new car was totaled. And since she was in a hurry to leave the house, she forgot to shut the stove. A fire broke out in the kitchen, and my whole house is gone. So, you see, Mr. Smithers, I think I might need to come back, uh, say, fifteen minutes or so late from lunch… so that I can… well… start getting things back in order. Okay?"

"I'm afraid I can't allow that, Joe, because if I do, then every single time the same things happen to another employee, I'll have to do the same for them! Sorry, Joe," replied a very corporate-minded Mr. Smithers.

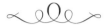

What do Mr. Smithers and Joe have to do with *chinuch* — or with Sukkos? Well, although Mr. Smithers is obviously a caricature of lunacy, what he represents, as an authority figure, sometimes comes into play in *chinuch*. Specifically he typifies the inability that some educators have in relating to an individual in a manner that takes into account his individuality. *Menahalim* and *mechanchim*, despite their typical and genuine *mesirus nefesh* for children, often display this ineptitude, failing to allow specific circumstances to affect the way in which they deal with *talmidim*.

A simple statement of the Seforno reveals a vital educational imperative. Yaakov Avinu gave a different blessing to each of the *shevatim* prior to his demise. Why could he not simply have given a single, collective *berachah* to all? Explains Seforno, "To each he gave a *berachah* designed according to his unique needs. Thus he gave monarchy to Yehudah, Torah to Yissachar and the *avodah* to Levi"(*Bereishis* 49:28). What made sense for one son does not necessarily make sense for another.

In *Chayei Olam* (part 1, ch. 3) we find a beautiful explanation of this. "People were created in various categories, depending on their particular characteristics and talents. For this is the honor of Hashem, namely, that [people] will serve Him in many ways, with each using that which is appropriate for him, according to his talents and experiences."

How wonderful it would be if *mosdos hachinuch* could adopt and perfect this position! In the educational climate that pervades our world, *mosdos* often adopt a "cookie-cutter" orientation, whereby the goal is to force all *talmidim* to conform to a single — and often confining — mold, and to produce cadres of graduates who resemble one another in almost every conceivable way. This seems to resemble what *Chazal* taught us about Sedom: if the body size of a guest did not conform to what was seen as the "correct" size, he would be either stretched or "trimmed" to correct his "deformity."

Bold as this may sound, then — especially in an age when we have become sensitized to issues of abuse — I would nevertheless suggest that stifling the individual character of any particular *talmid* can be considered worse than corporal punishment, for while the latter might inflict pain, which is temporary, the former can absolutely destroy, with permanent ramifications.

It is interesting to note, though, that this destruction produces a mutual impact. This is because when the *mechanech* does not take into consideration the specific nature of each *talmid*, and when he seeks to guide him in a way that misses the target, the *talmid* comes to feel alienated from his rebbi and eventually will dislike him and fail to accept upon himself the rebbi's *marus*, authority.

Consider the following words of the Slonimer Rebbe, the Nesivos Shalom, *zy"a* (*Nesivei Chinuch*, end of chapter 4). "One of the principal issues upon which success in *chinuch* depends is understanding the psyche of the child, whereby one needs to recognize his specific nature and moods. Only then, when the child sees that the rebbi understands him, he will love him, trust him and accept his authority upon himself. If [the rebbi] does not recognize the nature of the child, he might come to commit serious errors in *chinuch*."

(Truthfully, this is a pitfall that is easy to tumble into. Despite years of attempting to perfect my own cognition and application of this concept, a father recently shared that I may have failed to exercise this imperative with respect to his son several decades ago.)

Obviously, there can be no suggestion made that this should be the total orientation of the *mechanech* in dealing with his *talmidim*. One needs to manage a class, or a yeshivah: this requires well-planned regulations and techniques that will allow for the development of a group mentality and some degree of compliance and uniformity in both conduct and learning.

What one discovers, then, as is so common, is the importance of achieving balance. Thus we find in Rashi an explanation for why some of the expressions in the first passage of *Kri'as Shema* (*Shema* and *V'ahavta*) are repeated, though in plural, in the second passage (*Vehaya im shamo'a*). He declares, "*Azharah l'yachid, azharah l'rabbim* — [Moshe] warns them as individuals; but also as a collective entity." This is necessary because frequently a peculiarity in personality will require a leader to make concessions and dispensations for the individual, though these might represent a departure from the collective approach. After all, this is no more than an extension of "*eis la'asos laHashem,*" the idea that dimensions of specific situations might require, "*heifeiru Torasecha,*" departures from the strict rule of law. (See end of *Gittin, perek* 5.)

On Sukkos we are instructed, "*U'lekachtem lachem* — And you shall take." There are four *minim*, species, that we hold as we daven. The *esrog* is separate from the rest, as it symbolizes human perfection, or the *tzaddik*, as we find expounded in *meforshim*. It is the other three *minim*, however, that grab our attention. Each has its own "personality," its own particular blend of traits — including essential imperfections. At the same time, they are to be bound together. *Chazal* even teach that the *iggud*, the binding of the three, is obligatory. What emerges, then, is a balance between viewing each of the three *minim* as unique and between viewing them together as parts of a whole.

The obvious symbolism regarding people — especially *talmidim* — helps us understand how "*u'semachtem,*" and you shall rejoice, is achieved through the taking of the *minim*. There is a joy and solace on the part of an individual who knows that his personality is reckoned with by others, just as the Slonimer Rebbe wrote.

I will share a few case histories.

One *bachur* I know, a better-than-average *masmid*, was also uniquely talented in various ways. He was able and willing to put his gifts to use for the benefit of his yeshivah in areas of special programs for the student body. He was even called on by the *hanhalah* to do so on several occasions. However, when slight scheduling adjustments needed to be made in order to accommodate him, one *hanhalah* member felt challenged and incapable of making them. This turned into an impasse and an obvious source of friction. However, it could easily have been avoided.

One young lady I recall had difficulties in comprehension, something that made her overall learning experience somewhat negative. At the same time, she was an incredibly organized person and blessed with leadership skills. When a large-scale school-wide project was undertaken, and a single student was needed to position project displays and apportion topics to the student body, it was she who was selected. To say that she shone throughout that experience and beyond would be an understatement. The fact that she was also released from a small measure of her academic responsibilities only made the endeavor even more rewarding. Her gratitude was boundless to both *hanhalah* and to teachers who crafted her school experience to her needs, at least in part.

I recall a case of a girl who was extremely unhappy in her class — socially as well as academically — for she was on a learning level well beyond that of her classmates, although she was younger. Her parents were convinced that the only solution to her malaise would be for her to be accelerated — even in midyear. At first the *hanhalah* refused, as this step contravened school policy, and it would open the door to a rash of similar requests by others. On that basis, then, the parents' suggestion was rejected. However, the problem worsened, and after a Rav interceded, the school made the concession. Well, there were no additional requests made by others, and the young lady began to flourish, to smile and to become something of a star.

So, some stories conclude with happy endings. There are many, however, that are not so favorably resolved. So collective policies, rules, and dynamics are a necessity. However, it is just as true that the proverbial door needs to remain open — if only a crack — to accommodate the individual within the group.

Mr. Smithers didn't get it. Parents and *mechanchim* need to.

FRIENDS AND NOT PROJECTS

QUESTION: *For the past couple of decades, our children's yeshivos have implemented a wide variety of special mivtza'im — campaigns and programs — to effect changes in the values and lifestyles of our children. With no intent at skepticism, chas v'shalom, I really wonder if these are genuinely successful.*

It is no simple task to denigrate actions that appear to be steeped in goodness. However, sometimes such criticism is in fact justified.

A noted *mechanech* recently shared an experience he had several years ago. As a principal in a girls' school, he initiated an inclusion program for girls who had recently emigrated from the former Soviet Union. Their arrival in North America was the achievement of a visionary Torontonian philanthropist who wished to relocate promising young boys and girls in solid, North American yeshivah or Bais Yaakov settings. Obviously, when they came here, one of their most fundamental needs was schooling.

Therefore this principal gallantly chose to seize the moment and welcome the girls into his high school.

The initiative was a combination of *kiruv* — for these young ladies had seen very little Yiddishkeit back home — *chinuch*, and *chesed*. *Chesed*, on two counts: firstly, he would help provide for the newcomers; and secondly, he would in this manner guide the other *talmidos* in performing acts of lovingkindness for these spiritually (and, generally speaking, also financially) needy newcomers. It was a truly well-intended program, and the *menahel* was quite pleased — until one day.

He saw one of the immigrant students sitting in a corner crying. He approached her and inquired, "Why are you crying?"

Her response was, "I have no friends."

"Of course you do; you have many friends. Haven't so many people helped you in so many ways? There are those who paid the money for your ticket to get you here. And there are those who have brought you gifts of clothing and books to make you fit in. And what about those who invite you home for Shabbos? You have lots of friends."

"I am not their friend," the girl replied. "I am their project!"

Quite apart from the wisdom that the young lady obviously possessed in being able to express the idea so poignantly, the truth of her words rang loudly and clearly in the way it pertains to other *chinuch* issues, which brings us to the matter at hand.

What the American *chinuch* scene is undergoing for years now is a series of projects and awareness initiatives. To name a few: the Battle Against Internet Use, the Television Awareness Project, *derech eretz* and *shemiras halashon* programs, anti-"pop-culture" campaigns, anti-bullying programs, and more. To some extent, Jewish education has embraced the approach whereby projects spearhead the agenda of molding Jewish children and adolescents into loyal Jewish adults.

Certainly, as noted earlier, one cannot with integrity denigrate, or find fault with, any of these educational initiatives. They are essential endeavors and have earned an honorable spot in the world of *chinuch*. At the same time, there is arguably only limited practical success achieved by these endeavors, and it behooves us to decipher the reason.

At the outset it is worthwhile emphasizing the crucial difference between mere "edification" and between "internalization." The former is the act of imparting information, while the latter is the act of infusing it into the essence of another person. The imparting of information to a young person is a vital objective, to be sure, but the inculcating of an entire perspective into him or her is entirely and undoubtedly more vital.

In *Parashas Nitzavim*, Moshe Rabbeinu describes the accessibility of Torah to every Jew (*Devarim*, 30:14): "*Ki karov eilecha hadavar me'od, beficha u'vil'vavcha la'asoso* — This matter is very close to you, in your mouth and in your heart to do it." The Ibn Ezra explains how the three things — speech (*beficha*), heart (*u'vil'vavcha*), and action (*la'asoso*) — mentioned in this verse interact.

"The primary aspect of all *mitzvos* is the heart," he explains. "Some of them are subject to verbal reminders, to fortify the heart, and there are actions so that one will remember verbally." In other words, that which is the undisputed focus in our religious lives is the heart. That which has the greatest potential to impact upon the Jewish heart is Jewish speech. Actions are required, according to the Ibn Ezra, in order to precipitate verbalization; in and of itself, actions are more remote than speech in being able to make their mark upon the *neshamah* of an individual.

The conclusion to be drawn here is this: While it is too far to actually suggest that many of the special projects and campaigns that schools undertake to instill Jewish values into their students might smack slightly of being contrived, it is correct to infer that they might be somewhat ineffective as *chinuch* tools.

By comparison, what is more likely to succeed in achieving the goals of *chinuch* is the use of more traditional devices.

For instance, and although it is often repeated, one aspect that bears mention is "role-modeling." If a father whiles away his leisure time online, there is no reason to assume that his son will do otherwise, given the chance. If a mother unabashedly spends time on the phone speaking ill of others, there is no reason to assume that her daughter will distance herself from *lashon hara*. If a rebbi is quick to fly off the handle at his *talmidim*, they are not likely to be influenced by his *schmuess* about anger.

Another crucial method is simple discussion, by which Torah ideas are clarified and then internalized. The active and verbal involvement of *bachurim* or girls in the truthful discovery of Torah ideals is a means by which they are likely to accept them.

Ultimately *chinuch* needs to be pervasive, consisting of the portrayal of an all-inclusive lifestyle. School projects will do little to replace that primary approach.

Indeed, even if a yeshivah does utilize a "special project" in its bid to impart Torah values, its proponents must realize that the aim must be the heart. A successful project is measured neither by points, by "mitzvah notes," by test tubes being filled in red ink on a wall chart, nor by the prizes that were awarded to participants, by lists of *talmidim* who joined, or by the hype that often accompanies school activities. The success of a campaign is in its possibly having changed participants to their core.

There is perhaps an additional hint to this idea in the aforementioned context in *Parashas Nitzavim*. "*Lo bashamayim hi… v'lo me'eiver layam hi* — The Torah is not in the sky… nor is it across the sea." Torah is not to be sought through an appeal to the "sky" and the "sea" — to contrived educational venues and ingenious learning devices. Success is more down to earth.

To paraphrase the words of a young lady from the former Soviet Union, the teachings of the Torah want to be treated as true friends — and not as school projects.

CHINUCH GOING ON VACATION?

QUESTION: *After ten — and in some cases, eleven — months of school and hard work, our children go to a richly deserved vacation, some to camp, with others at different venues. It has been said that what a child learns in a year of yeshivah can possibly be undone during summer vacation. Is that an accurate portrayal of reality, or is it nothing more than an intimidating overstatement?*

Well, it may be intimidating, without being an overstatement. The concern for undoing a year of yeshivah has little to do with the material that the child studied — both *limudei kodesh* and *limudei chol* — but rather with the psychological and spiritual growth that the child has perhaps experienced during the school year and which might be imperiled during summer vacation.

The primary issue can be encapsulated with the adage that while a student can go on vacation, a Yid does not. In other words, those aspects of the individual that define his being a student, such as his academic activity, can indeed go on vacation, while those aspects that define his Jewishness, such as davening, cannot. Therefore, while there may be relaxation in the regimen of schedules and daily pressures, there cannot be a relaxation of behavioral standards.

More importantly, however, there must be no easing up in the need to control the subliminal absorption of ideas. Tremendous caution should be exercised regarding the sensory perceptions and the alternative value systems that might confront children while on vacation.

To fully comprehend this, it is important to commence with an understanding of the mechanical process of "inadvertent learning." The concept of friendship is an effective starting point.

The reason that the *mishnah* in *Avos* expresses the imperative for taking a rebbi with the word *aseh*, make ("*aseh lecha rav*"), while the one for taking a friend is expressed as *k'neh*, buy ("*k'neh lecha chaver*") — is that the latter is more crucial. The impact of friends supersedes that of teachers. One therefore needs to invest more effort in securing good friends than in searching for the perfect rebbi.

Among some *chassidim* it was, and is, the practice, when seeking a *berachah* from a *rebbe*, to ask for the special blessing of *chaveirim tovim*, good friends. This is grounded in the understanding of exactly how vital proper friends can be to spiritual development and ongoing well-being.

Indeed, in two places in Shas, two *Tannaim* were quoted as saying that they actually learned more from their friends than they did from their *rebbeim*. This comes as no surprise in light of the empirically proven reality, voiced by the Rambam at the start of *Hilchos Dei'os*, that the nature of man is to be drawn after his friends and neighbors in the manner in which he will conduct himself.

The reason that proper friendship is so crucial is that one absorbs much more within a setting that is relaxed. In such a setting, one's guard is down, making one extremely receptive. This can be referred to as "inadvertent learning." When the rebbi or *morah* stands at the front of the class and seeks to impart knowledge, ideas, or attitudes, there is an instinctive drive that impels the *talmid* or *talmidah* to possibly block it out in some measure. Good students are those who have become well-trained at overcoming that drive.

On the other hand, the non-challenging mood that laces friendships opens the field to inadvertent learning and the implantation of new thoughts. In the presence of one's friends, one's guard is down, and that is the beauty of friendship. But that is also the reason that one needs to be cautious.

In general, parents are wise to ascertain who their child's friends are, for they help to orient a child's development. Indeed, even later in life, a common "*shidduch*-information" question that gets asked is, "Who are his/her friends?" Such information describes the essential person.

The premise that relaxation promotes inadvertent learning is also what lies behind the use of parables as a powerful pedagogic tool. A narrative makes a deeper impression than an unadorned "thought," because the parable demands less strain in order to be internalized. It is more relaxing, or, to use the vernacular, "fun." This explains the propensity among contemporary public speakers to use dramatic stories at an increasing rate: they impact profoundly upon audiences and are more likely to be retained by them in the long term. This is also why the "*mashal*" is utilized so often in Midrashim, as well as by more contemporary luminaries, such as the Dubner Maggid and Rebbe Nachman of Breslov, *zecher tzaddikim livracha* and others.

The same holds true for anything that breeds the sense of relaxation; and vacation, by its very definition, represents the epitome of that very sense. Therefore the experiences that a child has while on vacation will probably have a more profound impact upon him than his experiences in yeshivah during the other ten or eleven months of the year. As a test of this principle, question your child to determine what some of his or her most memorable days over the past year — including summers — were. You will likely find that his vacation days come to the foreground in a vastly disproportionate or over-represented manner. His "color war break-out," for instance, might emerge as more eventful than his best *daf* of Gemara. Her graduation trip will stand out in her memory far more than the studies that preceded it.

The problem associated with all this is the fact that, in the words of the Lakewood Mashgiach, "We are living in a world of *hashchasah*," a world in which dehumanizing imagery, lasciviousness, cynicism, and corruption surround us on almost all sides. As long as the structured environment of the "*koslei beis midrash*" — the yeshivah and the Bais Yaakov — protect our youth (and even then the challenges abound!) we can be reasonably confident that the inadvertent learning will be of a positive kind. When vacation is upon us, however, the world of *hashchasah* comes caving in upon the heads of our youngsters.

The resulting imperatives, while perhaps obvious, bear repetition nevertheless.

Children who have lots of "free" time will possibly go "exploring." Vacation days — even if they are relaxing — need structure and schedule.

Camps may be expensive, but in terms of preserving the year-long gains of our *chinuch* systems, camps are without doubt the best instrument. The expense ought to be viewed as a worthwhile investment.

The cottage and the "country" do not ensure the propriety of inadvertent learning. In fact, depending on the specific venue, they might be worse than summer in the city. Colonies that provide an ambiance of modesty and of appropriate activity should be sought.

Tourist sites will inevitably be frequented by… tourists. Today's dress codes, or lack thereof, furnish young eyes with a *treif* smorgasbord. So, even when parents accompany their children on family trips, choices of sites to visit and hours to visit them must be made prudently.

In general, there is one principle that needs to be remembered when heading into vacation season. Make sure that, while the children themselves head to a hopefully relaxing and enjoyable vacation, their *chinuch* itself does not take any time off. In that way we can help safeguard that not only will ten or eleven months of yeshivah not come undone, but that the vacation can promote an enhancement for the year ending, and a sound preparation for the school season that lies ahead.

HAPPY TO BE HERE!

QUESTION: *What would be the single most important focus in motivating children to learn?*

At the outset it needs to be clarified that motivating factors for children of ordinary or better intellectual ability might be different from what they are for children contending with assorted challenges. Our question here centers on the former, that is, the common difficulty that adults have in motivating even mainstream children. To be sure, the difficulty arises from the fact that today there are so many diversions vying for a child's attention, and for his affections. The question, then, in other words, is this: "How can we make Torah study as attractive in a child's eye as the myriad flashy distractions that catch his fancy on the outside?"

JOY IN ACTION

We ought to always remember that enjoyment is one of mankind's chief motivators. Enjoyment can be utilized in this matter no less than in others. Let us see how.

In *Darkei HaChaim*, Rav Michel Yehudah Lefkovitch avers that a child's success in learning is contingent upon the *simchah* with which he learns. The reason is quite simple: "For then his cognition will be [invested] only in what he is learning; consequently he will more easily be able to comprehend," Reb Michel Yehudah writes.

The explanation of these words is crucial. An individual can simultaneously experience at least two levels of cognition: one is "first-order cognition" — in which one concentrates on a subject, an idea or an act etc.; and the other is "second-order cognition" — in which one focuses on the circumstances surrounding his first-order cognition. For instance, dealing with a *Tosfos* is first-order cognition, while a child's thinking of the hard time he is perhaps having dealing with the *Tosfos* is second-order cognition. Naturally, as in our example, second-order cognition bogs down the learning process.

So, if a child is not enjoying the learning, then besides contending with the Gemara or the Mishnah, he is also contending with a second-order cognitive load — namely, his agitation from experiencing something unpleasant and non-enjoyable. That extra mental task slows down his learning capacity. That, in turn, impedes his ability to achieve, and that, again in turn, negatively impacts upon his happiness level while learning. A vicious cycle!

Many years ago, a Jew pointed out to Rav Moshe Feinstein that the rampant *chillul Shabbos* among second-generation American Jews seemed to be inexplicable. After all, he noted, many of them had witnessed tremendous *mesirus nefesh*, self-sacrifice for Shabbos, on the part of parents who came across from Europe in the early 1900s. Thousands of Jews would have to find new jobs every Monday morning after being fired the previous Friday, when, fully aware of the consequences, they would announce to their employers that they would not come in to work on Shabbos. Why, asked the Jew, could such *mesirus nefesh* not safeguard the Shabbos observance among the children of those precious Yidden?

Reb Moshe answered that he believed it had to do with the attitude that was inadvertently conveyed by those fathers and mothers, even in the midst of their great self-sacrifice. Come Erev Shabbos, when a Jew would return home with the news that he was yet again unemployed because of Shabbos, he would have likely emitted a *krechtz* or a sigh, and he would have likely said such things as, "*Ess is shver tzu zein a Yid* — It is so difficult to be a Jew." When a generation of young Jews perceived that Shabbos observance was a source of anguish rather than a source of joy, when they heard parents say that Shabbos was an obstacle to success rather than a wonderful weekly oasis, they slowly became disenchanted with Shabbos, as well as with Torah observance in general. It was the lack of *simchah* that caused all the damage, explained Reb Moshe. If the focus would have been the enjoyment of Shabbos — not the sacrifice — the consequence would have been different.

By the same token, if a child sees his parents' joy over Torah study and mitzvah observance, he or she will associate these things with joy and excitement. Those are the best motivators.

JOY IN ANTICIPATION

However, there is another type of joy.

In the context of *Kabbalas HaTorah*, when our nation received its eternal legacy and mission, we read that *Bnei Yisrael* came to Sinai in the third month, "*bayom hazeh*," on *this* day. Rashi clarifies that the reference is to Rosh Chodesh. However, he continues by pointing out that grammatically it would seem more appropriate for the verse to read, "*bayom hahu*," on *that* day. What is the message inherent in "this day"? His explanation: The implication is that Torah should inspire fresh excitement in us at all times — just as if we had received it *this* day.

In fact, that concept is conveyed by *Chazal* in numerous passages in Torah. The passage here stands out, however, for there appears to be incongruity. The Kotzker Rebbe, in *Oholei Torah*, remarks that since it was the first day of Sivan, five days before *Kabbalas HaTorah*, what excitement could there have been? After all, they had no Torah yet.

The Kotzker Rebbe explains that in that context the focus of excitement was not Torah's text itself, but rather the prospect of receiving Torah. Besides the joy of actual learning, there needs also to be anticipatory *simchah* beforehand, like that felt by *Klal Yisrael* in *Midbar Sinai*. That preliminary joy is in many respects more crucial than what emerges later, simultaneous with the activity itself.

Children must detect from us that Torah is neither simply an academic pursuit nor a "school subject" alone. Through our example, they can learn that the excitement surrounding Torah permeates a Jew's entire existence.

In a similar vein, David HaMelech says (*Tehillim* 122:1), "*Samachti b'omrim li beis Hashem neileich*." He praises not merely those who have gone to the house of Hashem, but rather those who experience excitement before their imminent visit there. Well in advance, David HaMelech sang the praises of those (such as Diaspora Jews, according to *Radak* and others) who lived with the dream and the yearning of coming to the Beis HaMikdash. In that sort of excited anticipation lies the stuff of which motivation is made.

By extension, then, if a child sees that his father looks forward to his opportunities to learn, that perspective transforms into one of the child's own ideals. He will feel that learning is enjoyment.

A recurring question, then, that a parent needs to ask himself relates to the nature of things that cause him to be excited. Are those things spiritual pursuits and accomplishments or are they the physical and material goals that mankind often tends to celebrate?

Klal Yisrael arrived at *Midbar Sinai*. When they realized that they would receive the Torah in a few days, they sensed the monumental gladness that would actually become their preparation for Torah. That same frame of mind is what we are urged to emulate. We make ourselves students of Torah not by merely pushing ourselves towards excellence in its pursuit, but rather by conditioning ourselves to be happy about Torah study, before it and during it.

Predictably, parents will note that there is no greater motivator than that.

UPHOLDING THE TECH VIGIL

In case anyone is wondering, this chapter was written on a computer word processor, and it was submitted for print via email. So the writer of these lines would be hypocritical if he were to espouse that we must avoid all contact with and reliance on technology.

Obviously, though, to pretend that all is well in "Techland" would be both misleading and extremely dangerous.

When the illustrious Lakewood Mashgiach, Harav Mattisyahu Salomon met several years ago with the leading educators of Toronto's Jewish community, he averred that the devastation that is being incurred via the Internet is a new holocaust, a situation so deplorable that it must be viewed with extreme alarm and urgency by *mosdos haTorah*. Now, for an individual of such renown, deliberate with his choice of words, to refer to the crisis as a "holocaust" was at first rather startling. However, as the theme became exposed in its ugly detail, the choice of that particular word became crystal clear.

The Mashgiach outlined statistics pertaining to Jewish communities around the world, from Lakewood to Gateshead to

Yerushalayim. The gathering of more than a score of *menahalim* sat spellbound — and obviously distressed — as we heard case histories of families ripped apart and about young *bnei* and *bnos Torah* who fell victim to the ravages of the web, to the draw of chat rooms and to the temptations of freely accessible images.

"Social media" is a relatively new expression, denoting a variety of venues used to connect people via the Internet. The attractions of social media include the sharing of images, ideas, and opinions, open communication — even "networking" — among individuals who normally would not be linked — and more. It contributes to what is referred to as a well-rounded world view. Sounds good!

However, consider a telling comment from *Midrash* (*Bereishis Rabbah* 65:1). Among their descriptions of Eisav, *Chazal* write, "Eisav is likened unto the swine, which raises its hooves to say, 'See that I am clean!'" Much of what seriously threatens our well-being — as symbolized by Eisav — is innately deceptive, says the *Midrash*. As part of the manner in which the Creator fashioned all of existence, the swine was crafted as a paradigm of something that appears measurably "kosher" — after all, it has split hooves — but is decidedly not. Technology measurably falls into this category.

That is why since those days more than a decade ago, the war against technology has been waged with but limited success. Before long, social networking and social online media became all the craze — and sadly has remained so.

Statistics indicate that over twenty-five percent of American adolescents enter their social media sites at least ten times daily, with fully twenty percent of Internet use consisting of connection with so-called Facebook "friends." Teenagers have on average about 180 "friends" with whom they connect regularly. No youth needs that much social exposure — and none can handle it.

Then consider who these social contacts are. Can any youngster be certain of the moral integrity of all these "friends?" How often have we heard of predators that infiltrated into the lives of innocent youngsters with disastrous results. Surely, even if open disaster does not strike, parents would be foolish to assume that all relationships pursued through social networking are healthy.

A popular social media site, Twitter, has about 600 million accounts worldwide and nearly a half million new accounts added daily. Moreover, each day finds 55 million uncontrolled messages, known as "tweets," sent through the site. And what about the images uploaded and available through social media! There are 250 million photographs posted every day through the Facebook site alone. It is self-inflicted blindness for parents to imagine that all of what is available through social media is suitable for young eyes — or older eyes for that matter! Are we ready to jeopardize our children's modesty, the hallmark of *Am Yisrael*?

There's more. A survey conducted at Columbia University's National Center on Addiction and Substance Abuse a few years back revealed a link between teen consumption of social media and between substance abuse. It was shown that teens who use social media sites are five times more likely to use tobacco, three times more likely to use alcohol, and twice as likely to use marijuana, than those who do not.

If that's not enough, consider another social ill that emerged from social media: "*cyberbullying*." With the ability to hide behind the veil of anonymity, youngsters and adults alike post the most brazen, cruel, and hurtful comments about others. The defamation, the insult and the pain that are disseminated in blogs have caused untold psycho-emotional damage in targeted victims.

Back to the meeting with the Mashgiach! I was initially pleased to be part of a concerted effort to deal with this insidious problem, which has penetrated into even the most so-called *"heimishe"* circles and the most *"chareidi"* homes. The point at which I grew somewhat disheartened came only when I began to discuss the initiative with others who are *beyond* the realm of *mechanchim*. Some people expressed the notion that any effort to turn back the Internet tide would be "ridiculous because it has already become so much a part of our lifestyle, and it cannot be reversed." Then there were those who argued that with filters and controls the Internet can be tamed and should be made accessible to children (a solution that can border on the very flimsy). One person noted to me that "we have to be able to trust our children," and suggested that "we cannot supervise every moment of their lives."

More than one serious-minded layman argued that the reason that there are so many youths at risk in Torah-observant society these days is that they have been "cloistered" (his word), that is, overly sheltered and are unable to deal with the seductions of the world when they do meet up with them. We ought not even to consider the removal of Internet for that reason, he said. A misguided approach, to say the least: just think of which spiritual abyss that slippery slope might deposit our children at! The Rosh Yeshivah of Telshe, Chicago, Rabbi Avrohom Chaim Levin, has on more than one occasion suggested to audiences that a "kind" parent who gives an iPod or the like as a gift to his/her child might just as well give him a loaded pistol as a gift. This is serious business.

Fortunately, a tidal wave of awareness began to sweep through the Jewish world. *Gedolei Yisrael* entered the fray. Massive gatherings were convened and fiery rhetoric inspired Jewish hearts everywhere. TAG offices opened in many Jewish communities to guide individuals in adapting their computers to accommodate the best filters and surveillance tools. Yet, to use the imagery of an ancient Greek myth, each time a monstrous head was lopped off the beast, two new ones seemed to grow back in its place. So, just as great headway was made in the campaign against technology, the challenges have not truly been eliminated.

The long and short of it is that two endeavors need to continue in Jewish communities across the globe. Let us escalate the task of edifying parents about the grave danger in Internet use. The second is the imperative to take measures against those who have either allowed Internet use to taint the *kedushah* of their children or to those who refuse "on principle" to accept restrictions. As much as the path of pleasantness (*darkei noam*) is generally preferred over the path of stringent enforcement, there is the notion of "*eis la'asos laHashem*," a time when the sacred agenda of Hashem must be brought to the forefront.

The corporate world becomes increasingly dependent upon Internet. It therefore can be assumed that Internet cannot and will not become completely eradicated from the lives of Jews. The time has come, however, to tame the monster, to restrict its uses to what is absolutely necessary in the life of adults and to ensure that there is no danger to the innocence of our children. The potential holocaust that has already begun to descend makes this truly an *eis la'asos laHashem*.

BRANDY AND CAKE

QUESTION: *Despite the great amount of attention to the issue of at-risk youth, the tragedy of adolescents "going off the derech" seems to play out repeatedly. What can be done to halt the terrible tide?*

Generally, tragedies are not averted if we know little of where they come from. Every generation has its *nisyonos*, with those of one era often completely different from those of another. Rationally, in order for anyone to pass a test, he or she must understand the "questions." That is as true for a Chumash quiz as it is for the large tests — the *nisyonos* that face an entire generation. The attrition rate among our youth continues to be disturbing, indeed, but let us take a look at what might be the nature of the problem.

Consider first an illustration that varying winds and agendas impact differently upon different ages. The Gemara (*Yoma* 69b) teaches that the *yetzer*, the desire, for idolatry has subsided, whereas other desires still lurk at the door. Indeed, when did we last hear of a Jewish adolescent who left Torah for anther faith, *l'havdil*? If we do not hear about this, it is because that temptation is not an issue today.

Similarly, about one thousand years ago, the attraction of Islam began to yank young Yidden away from their tradition. This plague sucked so much commitment out of the Jews of North Africa that Jewish elders there were prompted to turn to R' Sherira Gaon, *zt"l*, of Pumbedisa, for help. The question posed? The elders needed to illustrate to their young that Torah tradition was authentic. So they asked, "How was the Mishnah written?" R' Sherira Gaon composed his famed "*Iggeres*" and saved untold numbers of Jews from becoming Muslims (*Rachmana litzlan*). That particular lure certainly is all but non-existent among our children today.

In a similar vein, well before a century ago, Jewish youth in Europe were being drawn to humanistic literature and to the broad cultural climate of the day. That was one of the primary forces that attacked Jews of the period. As was said of Mitzrayim, "There was no home in which there was no corpse." There was hardly a Jewish home into which the cultural bug had not infiltrated.

Then, decades later, the social philosophies and nationalism began to beckon to young Jewish hearts in a variety of shades and stripes, once again bringing near ruin to many Jewish families. Indeed, Agudas Yisrael, as well as the Bais Yaakov movement were among the more recent effective responses of Torah Jews to the corrosive spirit that threatened us then.

Still, we rarely if ever encounter today instances of young Jews bowing out of Yiddishkeit because of the overpowering pull of Jewish nationalism or the beauty of secular literature. So, when all is said and done, our challenges are new ones, and we need to know: which *nisyonos* affect us today?

At the risk of using common platitudes, I would urge that we recognize today's plague for what it truly is. The component of the person that is aroused by today's outside world is neither the intellect nor the vision of a greater world, neither alternative spiritual fulfillment nor lofty cultural experience. We live in the generation of the quick fix and of instant gratification. The basest aspect of the human condition is the focus of appeal in the world as a whole. This is reflected in today's leisure activities, in today's consumerism, in today's vernacular, and in today's music (even, at times, so-called "Jewish music"), among other things.

In brief, what beckons to our children from the world beyond is the perceived promise that myriad things will make them "feel good." And as the panorama of *olam hazeh* expands with its constantly new offerings of technology and varied pleasures, the *nisayon* of *chinuch* deepens.

The success of *mechanchim* today (and *baruch Hashem*, there is tremendous success all around us) lies in their facility to create within Torah at least the same gratification and "feel-good" sensation that young people predict they will obtain elsewhere. Torah acumen and lessons in proper *hashkafos* are crucial, but they need to be augmented in today's climate.

In truth, the Torah itself possesses an infinitely greater innate ability to satisfy the cravings of the Jewish soul than all of the feeble materialistic offerings presented by the world around us. David HaMelech wrote, "*Pikudei Hashem yesharim, mesamchei leiv*," Torah gladdens the [Jewish] heart. The problem that might exist, however, is that the heart has become damaged and does not function as it should. Such a Jewish heart might first need to be cured before it can appreciate the gift of *pikudei Hashem*.

One of the greatest Hungarian *tzaddikim* of the previous generation — many people still remember him, as he was *niftar* in 5684 (1924) — was R' Shayele Kerestirer. He was a *po'el yeshuos*, and there would be long lines of people (including non-Jews and even an occasional priest!) seeking his advice and help daily. In his earlier years, a known *mekubal* visited R' Shayele and offered to teach him secrets of *kabbalah* with which to restore a person's soul and help him.

R' Shayele responded, "Thank you, but I use an entirely different approach. When a man comes to see me with a troubled heart, hungry, and depressed, I begin by offering him a glass of brandy and a piece of cake. Then I give him some money, and, instantly, his soul is restored."

Was R' Shayele suggesting that the methods of the *mekubal* were either inappropriate or ineffective? No. What he meant to say is, quite simply, that the secrets of Torah cannot penetrate a damaged heart. The initial cardiac cure is the priority at hand; the wonders of Torah need to be introduced by a Rebbe who understands that fundamental truth.

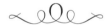

In terms of a practicum, what all this means is the following: In an ideal setting, nothing more than Torah is required to ensure that our children will remain loyal both to the practice and study of Torah. Often, however, settings are less than ideal. A child might experience some sort of learning difficulty. Or, a child might be subjected to abuse — either at home or at school. Or, a child may be lacking confidence because there is no *shalom bayis* at home. Or, a child may experience material deprivation — not enough sleep or food, for instance. Indeed, there are countless things that may compromise the well-being of a child's heart. Then, he discovers that the world outside tempts him with things that will make him feel better — unchallenged, seemingly at peace. Therein lies the danger.

Mechanchim and parents must both ensure that today's child will not be motivated to be lured away. Variations on the simple but vital approach of R' Shayele Kerestirer will go a long way to ensure greater allegiance to Yiddishkeit.

Both the *neshamah* and the common sense of our children, if unfettered by the combination of unhappiness and foreign temptations, will practically ensure that today's tragedy of attrition will start to subside.

THE CHACHAM WANTS TO BE HERE!

QUESTION: *Why is it that some children — more so than others — look forward to coming home from school?*

The answer might be connected to "ambiance." Let us use Pesach as a point of embarkation.

The opening *mishnah* in *Maseches Rosh Hashanah* tells us that there are four *Rashei Shanim* — four yearly commencements recognized by the Torah. However, there might in fact be a fifth one — though it would obviously not enjoy the same stature as the other four. I refer, in particular, to Pesach, which can be viewed as perhaps serving as a *"Rosh Hashanah l'chinuch."* Pesach is a time when we naturally fix our gaze on *chinuch habanim*.

Consider the varied roles that children play in the proceedings of the *Seder*. First, for weeks before, they have been studying the *halachos* of Pesach in school, as well as varied *pirushim* on the Haggadah; they wait with bated breath to share their learning, as well as their artistic innovations and Pesach projects, at home. Secondly, the halachah stipulates that we perform an array of acts to stimulate the child's participation and his desire to ask about the uniqueness of this Yom Tov. Thirdly, the halachah states that a child who has even a minimal understanding of *Yetzias Mitzrayim* should be given a cup with which to fulfill the *mitzvah* of *arba kosos*. And of course the child is placed in the limelight by reciting the four *kushiyos*. Indeed, the Haggadah itself finetunes our *chinuch* awareness by teaching us that the Torah speaks about four kinds of sons, each of whom needs a customized approach.

Additionally, we engage in a "find the *afikomon*" ritual with our children in order to pique their interest and excitement. Clearly never during the Jewish calendar's cycle of events is the *chinuch* of children placed so front and center as it is on Pesach, the *Rosh Hashanah l'chinuch*!

Inevitably, then, there is a myriad of crucial related lessons to be discovered in the rich text of the Haggadah. Indeed, the very mitzvah of *haggadah* itself, that is, "*v'higadeta l'vincha*," leads one to focus on the education of his children. So let us pinpoint one of the lessons found in the account of the *arba'ah banim* to find a thought relevant to the issue at hand.

That which sets the *rasha* apart from the other sons is his use of the word, "*lachem*." He asks, "*Mah ha'avodah hazos lachem* — What does this ritual offer *you*?" In his use of this word, he has isolated himself from the people, thus deserving a firm rap on the mouth. If only he were more like the *chacham*!

Consider, however, the text of his wise sibling's question. "*Mah ha'eidos… asher tzivah Hashem Elokeinu eschem* — What are these laws and ordinances which Hashem has commanded *you*?" Note that the *chacham* seems to commit the exact same verbal *faux pas* as his sinister brother. Why, then, does he merit the accolade of "*chacham*"?

In fact, this question is raised by the *Daas Zekeinim Mi'Baalei HaTosfos* in the commentary to *Devarim* (6:20). His answer contains an important key to understanding some nuances of character that are so telling in life as a whole.

That which sets apart the *chacham* from the *rasha* is the simple fact that the wise son uses the term "*Elokeinu*," our Hashem. One can hardly accuse the wise son of isolating himself from the *klal* if he includes himself religiously by referring to Hashem as "our Hashem." Therein lies the crucial difference.

The question that begs to be asked, though, is this: if the *chacham* does in fact view himself as part of the *klal*, why does he then proceed to utter the word, "*eschem*," which is exclusionist? Is he not contradicting himself?

The reason, explains the *Daas Zekeinim*, is that insofar as the son was not present at the time of *yetzias Mitzrayim* and *Kabbalas HaTorah*, he senses a degree of alienation from the Torah, recognizing that his father/ mother/ rebbi/ *morah*/ mentor is one step closer to the source and must therefore be more in tune with it, empowered with a stronger sense of identity with it. So paraphrasing what the wise son asks his father, it is this: "As one whose footings in Torah are stronger than mine, can *you* tell me what it is all about?" The *chacham* feels that he belongs to the *klal*. His "*eschem*" signifies merely that he recognizes that he still has much to learn. He seeks to be at home within his Torah study.

As simplistic as it sounds, then, the father must first have a *chacham* before him, prior to his being able to answer the response that is geared to the *chacham*. By the same token, in terms of the sequence of events, the rebbi must teach only *after* he has successfully fostered in his *talmidim* the predisposition that Torah is where they feel at home. That is much more primary, or fundamental, than the learning itself.

This is reminiscent of what the Gemara teaches us (*Berachos* 10b) about Shmuel HaNavi, when it speaks about his hometown and comments the obvious, "For there is his home." Was it not obvious that Shmuel's home is where his hometown is? The Gemara explains that wherever Shmuel HaNavi went, "*ki sham beiso*," there was his home. And while there are varied interpretations of these words, a particularly beautiful one is that "home" for a righteous person does not necessarily have the single, customary connotation that we are all familiar with. A righteous person can be at home elsewhere too — in his yeshivah, in his *beis midrash*, in his *shtiebel*, and in his school.

In the case of a young child, it should be considered the task of his rebbi to advance this feeling in his *talmid* and that it should be cultivated in the school as a whole. Home will always be home for a child, but there is tremendous benefit in a rebbi or a *menahael* promoting the perception that there is nearly the same degree of warmth and acceptance in school as there is at home. The promotion of this mood is ideally the most fundamental goal of a *mechanech* — even prior to actually teaching anything.

Predictably, the most prominent factor in understanding why some children clamor more than others to return home is determining to what extent the child feels alienated and uncomfortable at school. There is no question that an atmosphere that is devoid of bullying, of embarrassment, of put-downs, and of overt censure — whether these emanate from peers or from the adults in a child's school life — will fashion a school experience by which the child is more than likely to feel that he has a genuine second home.

Such an environment is most likely to generate a cadre of genuine *chachamim*, and not, *chas v'shalom*, anything other, for the *chacham*, as we have noted, is the son (or daughter) who wants to be here.

MORE THAN A REPLACEMENT: A REAL FATHER

QUESTION: *Each summer I take leave of talmidim with whom I have developed a kesher over the year, and I find this emotionally taxing. I'm wondering if that feeling is common — or even normal.*

When a child leaves home, parents suffer from the separation more than the child will. This is the natural order in the parenting world. Almost as instinctive as that sensation is the feeling a rebbi might have when he faces the reality of his *talmidim* leaving him.

To begin with, there are ample parallels between a father and a rebbi in the words of *Chazal*, and several of these sources indicate this notion of *ahavah*, love, that a rebbi will (hopefully) feel towards his *talmidim*.

A simple comparison is this. *Chazal* teach (*Sanhedrin* 105b), "*Bakol adam miskanei, chutz mibno v'talmido* — A person is naturally envious of others, except for his son and his *talmid*." The reason is simple: both the *talmid* and the son are extensions of the individual, as a result of the "investment" that is made into them. A person will hardly be envious of himself! Hence, one is joyful with the successes and achievements of children and *talmidim*.

The rebbi's bond, however, can be even more intense: the father invests materially in his son, while the rebbi invests spiritually. *Chazal* are not merely telling us here what a rebbi "should feel," but rather what predictably he does feel.

We find reinforcement of this concept in the words of the Maharal. In *Nesivos Olam, Nesiv HaTorah*, chapter 8, the Maharal writes, "The *talmid* and his rebbi have an extreme connection and bond together. There is no other connection that is as strong as the connection between a *talmid* and a rebbi."

Reading this, one assumes that the Maharal refers to the relationship between a rebbi and *talmidim* who are older — adults or near adults. How surprising it is then to find, a few lines later, "It is certain that the adult [student] does not have the same bond to the rebbi — and he may not even have the same classification as '*talmid*' — as does the child who is more profoundly linked to his rebbi."

The reasoning of the Maharal is this: the older one grows, the more he becomes galvanized in his thinking and in personality, and thus the less likely he will be a "*mekabel*." The younger a person is, the more he absorbs the impact made by the adults in his life. Hence the rebbi of younger *talmidim* has a tremendous effect on the very formation of the *talmid*. That is the basis for a relationship that is deep and everlasting.

A beautiful story is told of the holy Chozeh of Lublin. He was once traveling with two of his *chassidim*. When the group came to a crossroads, the wagon driver asked the Chozeh which direction they should go. The Chozeh, curiously enough, replied that the driver should simply let the horses go where they choose to.

Hours later, the wagon and its passengers arrived in a small town. Due to the lateness of the hour — it was Erev Shabbos — it appeared that they would have no choice but to spend Shabbos in the town. The *chassidim* asked the Rebbe, "But where shall we have the *Shabbos seudos*?" The Rebbe answered, "We will simply go to shul tonight; townspeople will undoubtedly invite us to spend Shabbos in their homes; there is nothing to worry about."

Sure enough, after davening, two local Yidden had invited the two *chassidim* to their homes; the Chozeh himself, however, remained uninvited. Just as the shul had emptied out of its *mispallelim* and the Chozeh was resigning himself to spending the night — and Shabbos itself — in the *beis midrash* alone, he noticed an old Yid sitting in the corner concluding his davening. When the elderly man noticed the Chozeh, he approached him and offered, "Reb Yid, I have very little at home to offer you, but whatever I do have I would be more than happy to share with you." The Chozeh accepted the invitation.

Indeed, the home was little more than a shack, and the *seudas Shabbos* was as humble as could be, but in the mind of the Chozeh, this was a beautiful *seudah* — laced as it was with *divrei Torah* and *zemiros*. His host asked him, "Where are you from?"

"Lublin," answered the Chozeh.

Wide-eyed with excitement, the host asked, "Lublin? Did you ever meet the famous *tzaddik*, Reb Yaakov Yitzchak, the one they call the Chozeh?"

The Chozeh asked, "Why do you ask? Are you in any way connected to the Chozeh?"

The host answered, "When the Chozeh was a child, I was his rebbi, and I remember that he was special in many ways. I have longed to see my former *talmid* for many years. In fact, each day I ask that the Creator keep me alive long enough so that I'll have the *zechus* of setting my eyes upon him once again."

The Chozeh then recognized his rebbi, and when he identified himself, the two enjoyed an incredibly beautiful Shabbos together. Sunday morning, the Chozeh took leave, and he and his *chassidim* set out for their return journey. Shortly after their departure, though, the Rebbe told his *chassidim*, "Tell the driver to turn around. I wish to deliver a *hesped* at a very special *levayah*." Sure enough, that is what happened.

Predictably, numerous lessons can be derived — some about the Chozeh himself. For our context, however, the story's beauty lies in its illustration of the profound love that the rebbi had for his *talmid* — to the point where merely seeing him became his sole reason to live.

In *Siach Sarfei Kodesh*, one finds that the Chiddushei HaRim, *zy"a*, in uncustomary style, shared numerous personal reminiscences at one particular Friday night *tisch*. One of these concerned the renowned *sofer*, Reb Moshe of Pshevorsk, author of *Ohr Pnei Moshe*. Prior to his becoming a scribe, Reb Moshe had been for years a *melamed*. The Chiddushei HaRim said of him that he used to infuse great *yiras Shamayim* into his *talmidim*. He would immerse himself in the *mikveh*, recite *Tehillim*, and daven often, all for the success that he wished his young charges to have in their learning and in their growth in performance of *mitzvos*. The Chiddushei HaRim concluded, "If only I could find a *melamed* like that today, I myself would become his *talmid*."

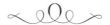

There is little doubt that this is the paradigm of the true

melamed: the ideal rebbi is one who feels love for his *talmidim* and emotional concern that they shall succeed. And while the degree to which that is the norm might be somewhat rare today, I have no doubt that the very best *rebbeim* in today's world of *chinuch* do indeed harbor such feelings. Without doubt, that is the goal to which all should aspire.

In a famous address by Rav Yitzchak Hutner on the topic of *chinuch* (reprinted in the end of *Pachad Yitzchak* on Shavuos) we find some of the most fundamental truths of *chinuch*, including the concept that is most pertinent to our discussion.

"*Chinuch* was always built on the axiom that one must receive Torah from the very same source from which one receives life itself. That is why Torah had always been received from one's father, as the Gemara (*Bava Basra* 21a) states." The fact that, following the lead and the insightful vision of Yehoshua ben Gamla, *Chazal* implemented the replacement of the father with the "*beis rabban*" — ostensibly, the yeshivah — was a necessary "adjustment," explained Rav Hutner, to a sad reality — the weakening of the father's role in the *mesorah* of Torah.

At the same time, he continued, "If the Sanhedrin ever made a *takanah* for future generations, one that was intended to endure until the end of days, that *takanah* in turn injected into *Klal Yisrael* all of the strengths and potentialities that would be required for the fulfillment of that very *takanah*." Thus, Rav Hutner says, the classical rebbi through the generations must have been imbued with the attribute of fatherliness to enable him being the proper source and transmitter of Torah to young *talmidim*.

Again, this is much more than a prescriptive statement that "advises" or "encourages" a rebbi to emulate the father, or to become something of a father figure. It is a statement of essential and objective truth. The rebbi, as far as his task of teaching Torah to his students is concerned, *is* a father. (It is little wonder, then, that Rav Hutner, with his keen understanding of this notion, was in fact revered as a veritable father by his *talmidim* — arguably more so than other Gedolei Torah of the time.)

So, all things considered, the emotional drain that a rebbi might feel when he says good-bye to his "children" at the end of the school year is not only normal — and proper — but the greatest evidence of a rebbi serving *Klal Yisrael* according to the ideal. If, on the other hand, a rebbi on that last day of school sees his *talmidim* leave and feels either a sense of "*Baruch shep'tarani*," or even plain ambivalence, that might be cause for concern.

IN PURSUIT OF EXCELLENCE

First it must be stated that excellence is a recognized virtue. Instinctively we all share reverence for it. We look with awe at great *talmidei chachamim*; we view respectfully the most accomplished doctors, albeit differently; even those who have achieved wealth are regarded with measured admiration. The list goes on, but the common denominator is this: we revere excellence. Most dream of achieving it in their lives and equally wish to see it accomplished by their progeny.

Yet, the anecdote comes to mind of a father who expresses his wishes to — and about — his son. "My son, I want you to grow up and be a success." To which the son responds, "No, Tatty, I do not want to be a success — I want to be just like you!"

So, a question surrounding the idea of "excellence" in Torah learning has confounded parents for a long time: Can we expect excellence in our children if we do not portray it ourselves? (In a similar vein, one thought that plagues some *mechanchim* is, "I push *talmidim* towards being *metzuyanim*, while I myself was not a *metzuyan* as a child." It is a seeming problem of duplicity.)

A second question: how can we promote the pursuit of excellence among children without incurring the risk of bruising their young egos?

The reality is often far removed from the lofty aspirations. Indeed, if excellence were ordinary, it would cease to be viewed as "excellence." Naturally, most of us fall short of the plateau that is naturally reserved for minorities. I am not the best writer, and most readers are not necessarily the best at whatever they may do. Yet, we aspire to have the best children. But how?

Obviously, in the real world of *chinuch*, we make peace with mediocrity even as we simultaneously aspire for excellence. Rav Aharon Leib Steinman was once asked whether there can be justification for removing the weakest student from a class on the pretext that he holds up the rest. His response was no, for as soon as the so-called weakest is removed, the next lowest will simply slide down to fill the position, and the process becomes endless. Children and adults who are not *metzuyanim* are part of our world! So how does this jive with dreams of excellence?

We must understand the basis upon which we promote the pursuit of excellence in our children if we fail to represent it in our own lives.

A *gadol b'Yisrael* once said that the telltale sign of what parents cherish is seen in what their children cherish — and that may not even coincide with what parents actively portray. If parents place the highest premium on financial success and dream about it, children will adopt that same goal. This has nothing to do with whether the parent has actually achieved wealth.

In *Nesiv HaTorah*, the Maharal explains *Chazal*'s statement that

Torah will emanate from the children of the poor in the following way: it is not the poverty itself that promotes Torah among the children of the poor; it is just that poverty generally indicates aspirations more spiritual than tangible. Since the aspirations and dreams of parents form the legacy passed to children, *Chazal* deduce that Torah will likely emanate from *bnei aniyim*. The same can be said regarding excellence in Torah.

We can with integrity promote excellence in children if, and only if, we cherish it ourselves. If excellence in Torah tops the list of our own priorities, we may even fail to actively exemplify it, although we do need to try. In that event children will internalize the priority by osmosis. It is only when we throw children mixed signals — idolizing one type of pursuit while paying lip service to another for the supposed benefit of our children — that they might come to view excellence in Torah as a vacuous dream.

That then becomes both the mode and justification for promoting and expecting excellence from our children. First, dream about it; aspire to it; seek to achieve it. Then it can be promoted to children with integrity.

This, then, leads us to the second question and the issue of how to actually advance excellence — in ourselves and in our children.

In a word, one must strive to be excellent — and not to emulate excellence. In the opening passage of *Shemos Rabbah*, the Midrash compares us to stars, averring that just as the Almighty loves each star as unique, so does He love us. Consider the nature of stars as opposed to that of the moon. The latter is a light source, but only by reflection of another. Stars are sources of light in themselves: each one shines *essentially* and need reflect nothing else.

The Yid is created as a star, able to shine brightly, but the light of each is unique to him or her, being inherent to him or her.

Although we can aspire to be like others — in fact we hope to be like *gedolei Yisrael*, and we are encouraged to say "*Masai yagi'u maasai...*" (When will our actions reach those of our ancestors?) those goals are meaningful only if they are *essential* to us. Imitating excellence is a nearly empty pursuit.

Consequently, excellence is truly pursued if it facilitates the use of the true essence of the individual. When it comes to Torah study, then, some have the innate tendency for *bekius*, mastery of large amounts of material, while others are better suited to delving in greater depth. Some of us might find ourselves naturally leaning towards studying halachah, while others might feel greater affinity for *hashkafah*. There just can be excellence in one area while there may be none in others. The promotion of excellence in an individual is predicated upon getting each to shine brightly for what he or she is — without feeling compelled to emulate others.

Consider that R' Yochanan ben Zakkai had five renowned disciples. While one (R' Elazar ben Arach) might have outshone the others, the rebbi found the excellence of each as something separate and unique. Thus did he recount the praises of each (*Pirkei Avos* 2:11). When he asked for their views, the rebbi summarily announced that the responses of R' Elazar ben Arach were more worthy. Yet, the views of all five were recorded for posterity (ibid., *mishnah* 13–14).

We also find that the *sheleimus*, perfection, of the *Shivtei Kah* coincided with their ability to overcome their envy of Yoseph. Only when they recognized that each individual had his own essence, and that it was unlike that of any other person, did they cease to view Yoseph enviously. That opened the door to their achieving excellence. (See *Sfas Emes, Vayigash.*) Ponder the ultimate greatness of Yehudah and Levi, and find it obvious that greatness did not hinge on some nebulous ambition of imitating Yoseph.

So it is with all people. While there needs to be universality in the manner in which parents treat children and in the curricular approaches to *talmidim*, there needs to be an allowance for each individual to excel innately. In some cases, that will open the door to alternate kinds of development. If a boy has a strong penchant for davening, but does poorly academically, encourage him to be an excellent "davener." Recognize that excellence, and his self-image might well strengthen and he might be more motivated to expend effort in the other areas. If a girl loves *chesed* activities but dislikes her studies, capitalize on what she is. She can first excel in *chesed* and her enhanced sense of self-worth may well spill over into the more challenging aspects.

Cherish excellence in your own lives. Then, nurture it in your children by finding the manner in which each "star" shines brightly.

MISBEHAVIORS — OPPORTUNITY KNOCKING
TOOLS FOR BUILDING STRONG JEWISH CHARACTER

In many ways the classroom is a microcosm of the world. It is a miniature venue in which a young person can be taught various life skills that are applicable later in life, within the broader venues of society. The notions of social contract and the rule of law, the complexities of interpersonal relationships, the value of an industrious work ethic, respect for authority and authority figures — these are among the "life skills" that can be imparted to students through their schooling experience.

It is this last concept, however, that has pertinence here, I contend that the awe and honor that a child develops for his rebbi or *morah* can well become manifest later in life as the awe and the honor that he or she will feel, as an adult, towards the Almighty.

In fact, *Chazal* have taught ample lessons regarding this: the obligations that we have to show respect for and to fear authority figures in this world are merely instruments by which we cultivate *yiras Shamayim*. We are taught: "*mora rabach k'mora Shamayim,*" one ought to fear his teacher as he would fear Hashem. Also, we find in the words of *Chazal* that Hashem considers *kibud av va'eim* to be equivalent to *k'vod Shamayim*. We even find that *malchus*, monarchy, in this world was advanced by the Creator only as a means of facilitating the proper appreciation for *Malchusa d'Rakia*, the Kingdom of Heaven.

So, insofar as the classroom is a microcosm of the world — indeed a breeding ground for many of the standards and principles that will be deployed by children in their later years — the need to utilize the yeshivah in the most productive manner possible cannot be overstated. The way in which a child evolves in school will probably have permanent impact.

In particular, the corollary of one of the above concepts is worthy of the limelight here. If it is true that a child is likely to shape his relationship to the Creator through the manner in which he relates to his rebbi, then it would follow, for that reason alone, that the rebbi is compelled to emulate the *Ribbono shel Olam* as much as possible in order to facilitate this.

(In truth, we are familiar with the imperative of "*Mah Hu rachum, af atah rachum*," and so on, that we are obliged to follow in Hashem's *middos* in general. However, in this current context we speak of that imperative in a specialized sense, namely, in terms of its being a teaching tool.)

We are well advised, then, to inspect a central theme — *mechilah*, forgiveness — and translate what we derive from that inspection into an appropriate pedagogic technique. Based on how we perceive *mechilah* working in our link to Hashem, we can formulate the correct approach toward forgiveness to our *talmidim* — indeed, to our own children.

Part of the process of maturation is the high incidence of infraction — certainly in the first decade of a child's schooling. Whereas the inclination to do what is good (*yetzer tov*) is infused into the individual at the time of his or her becoming *bar* or *bas mitzvah*, the shady inclination to do wrong (*yetzer hara*) is activated at birth (*"l'pesach chatas roveitz"*). Children, as they grow, will — often clumsily — commit one infraction after the other and often trounce upon the sensitivities and assumptions of the adults in their world — parents and *mechanchim* alike. Those adults are easily tempted into becoming impatient, angry, intolerant, and punitive. Correctly viewed, however, infractions are in reality opportunities for growth and can be used productively.

Consider the words of Rabbeinu Yonah at the beginning of *Shaarei Teshuvah*. "Among the kindnesses that Hashem has done for His creations is that He prepared for them the way to rise from the pit of their actions and to flee from the trap of their sins." *Teshuvah* is not merely the chance to erase, then, as is commonly believed: it is the chance to *rise* and to build momentum — so that one can actually *flee*. Certainly we must not urge our *talmidim* to err in order that they can avail themselves of this chance. However, seeing as children's infractions are all but inevitable, the *mechanech* is wise to guide his young charge to make the most of the opportunity.

If anger and impatience will play a role at all, they must be feigned, used theatrically, only as a pretext for guiding the child along the path of self-improvement. Let the child rise and let him or her flee!

The verse "*Hashem chevel nachalaso*," suggests that the link between Hashem and His people is likened unto a rope. R' Meir of Primishlan once explained this analogy. When a rope becomes severed, it can be repaired by tying a knot. The result however, is that the rope will be shorter; the distance between the two ends is reduced. By the same token, human infraction severs the link with Hashem. But when the "rope" becomes knotted through the individual's remorse and self-improvement, the distance between Creator and creation is less than it was before. Again, this is not a license to sin (for even Yom Kippur is unable to eradicate the sins of one who says "*echeta v'ashuv*") but a blessing latent within the sin.

Extending this to the classroom is not difficult. The building up of a child's character, of his self-confidence and of his determination to behave properly is a goal that can be easily achieved following the prerequisite dialectic of "infraction-rebuke-guilt-remorse." The child must not be made to wallow in his guilt and remorse, for they are destructive states of mind. Instead, when a child has strayed, he must be disciplined reasonably. When that has been done, however, the rope between *mechanech* and *talmid* then becomes repaired so that the child can benefit greatly. He can now be brought closer to the rebbi — as well as to all that the rebbi represents — than he might have been otherwise.

Naturally, there are sometimes violations that are so immense that the paradigm for *mechilah* needs to be more complex and lengthy. Retribution is a multi-faceted course: just as is the case regarding our own sins against the Creator, some indiscretions are more serious than others and need to be treated accordingly. A great deal of common sense — and often a *shailas Chacham* — must be exercised in these cases. The fundamental truth, however, is that for most misbehavior, it is the role of the *mechanech* to manipulate the incident as a facilitator for his student's growth.

"*Ki vayom hazeh yechaper aleichem l'taher eschem mikol chatoseichem* — For on this day [Yom Kippur] Hashem will atone upon you, to cleanse you *from* your sins." One might suggest that the cleansing is best achieved when it is achieved "*mikol chatoseichem*," from within the dialectic of sin and remorse. The cleansing that follows it is monumental.

So is it in the world and so is it in its microcosm, the classroom.

CREATING AN AIR OF INTERACTIVITY

QUESTION: *There are cases of children or talmidim who take absolutely no active part in the learning — not even in classroom discussion. On the other hand, there often appears to be a level of interest on their part. What can be done for such children?*

Even in prison, Rebbi Akiva needed no convincing regarding the merit of teaching Torah. When a disciple attempted to prompt him, Rebbi Akiva responded, "*Yoser mimah she'ha'egel rotzeh linok...* — Even more than the calf's desire to be fed is the cow's desire to feed it."

Now, Rebbi Akiva could certainly have conveyed that idea without resorting to that particular metaphor by simply stating that a rebbi seeks to teach more than the *talmid* seeks to learn. Why was there a need to borrow symbolic language from the animal world? In truth, if the Tanna expressed himself in that fashion, it is, I believe, because he pointed to an instinctive drive that humans have — a natural urge so basic that it can be likened unto the animal "desire" mentioned in the metaphor. That instinctive drive is the sharing of one's learning, one's ideas, one's knowledge and opinions.

This does not apply only to *mechanchim*, because the complex of instincts does not become altered merely because an individual chooses to become a teacher. Human instinct transcends vocational boundaries. And the urge to be verbal is a basic human drive.

The essence of the *nishmas chaim* that Hashem imbued into man is the "*ruach memallela*," a spirit of speech, according to *Targum Onkelus*. This means that, as noted, man has a natural urge to express himself. Why then do some people refrain from doing so? It is because varied circumstances surrounding the individual act as effective barriers to his being verbal. Those circumstances could include fear of saying the wrong thing, shyness, modesty, speech impediments, age, apathy regarding the topic at hand, and many more (and in Rebbi Akiva's case: *disciplina Romana*!). One also commonly finds that a child who refrains from verbal participation at school can actually be quite verbal at home. The underlying and innate human drive, therefore, is this: the human being wishes to be heard. It is important for parents and *mechanchim* to remember this when attempting to deal with the non-active participant.

In terms of a teaching practicum, we know that there are different kinds of learners. Auditory learners absorb information mostly from hearing; visual learners, from seeing; and kinesthetic learners, from tactile experiences. Within the traditional world of transmitting Torah to children, auditory and visual skills are the faculties that are used most. Curiously, however, some secular pedagogues suggest that even when such a time-honored style is used, the teacher's voice should not be heard more than fifteen percent of the time! That means that students' voices should be heard the rest of the time (besides a possible time allotment for silence!).

Now, in a Torah venue, that breakdown of time is unrealistic, since the rebbi's active part requires much more than fifteen percent of the time. At the same time, without our here quantifying the issue with a specific percentage, I would suggest that many *mechanchim* do monopolize class time. This could impact upon non-active participants. A rebbi who has difficulty eliciting active participation from a child might be spending too much time speaking, or doing *"frontal teaching."* The more common it is for the voice of *talmidim* to fill the air, the more likely it will be for the more reticent child to be brought out in the course of time, as the child will increasingly recognize that active participation forms a vital component of his overall role. Though not a guarantee, this is one of several devices to be deployed.

Indeed, a thought forwarded by the Rebbe R' Henoch of Aleksander is both topical and very fundamental.

In the *Haggadah shel Pesach*, we read of the *"she'eino yodeia lish'ol,"* the last of the four sons concerning whom the Torah instructs the father. Whatever the issue is that impacts upon this fourth son — whether it is apathy, a poor self-concept, or a sense of being disjointed from the proceedings of the themes of Pesach — he is the classical case of a child who is a non-active participant. He will not take the initiative to ask; so the Haggadah urges the father to break the ice: *"At pesach lo —* You open the conversation."

But why the feminine pronoun *"at"* instead of the masculine *"atah"*? There are numerous answers to this oft-asked question. The Rebbe Reb Henoch posed the following interpretation: As we find in numerous sources, the feminine nature is to be a "*mekabel*," more passive, while the masculine tendency is to be a "*nosein*," more active. The Haggadah instructs the father regarding the means with which to reach the "*she'eino yodeia lish'ol.*" Begin the conversation, but maintain the role of "*at*," that is a passive stance, as connoted by the feminine pronoun.

The message, then, is "Manipulate the conversation, but do not monopolize it; induce him to vocalize." The frontal technique will not work with this son, while the interactive one well might. Do not see yourself as a "lecturer," or a "*maggid.*" Instead, see yourself as a learning manipulator. Ask the child his view, and show respect for it. Pretend not to know some "answers" that you suspect he might know; this could induce him to open up. Use facial gestures that will display genuine interest in his thoughts.

The etymological source of the word "educate," is the Latin infinitive "*ducare*," meaning to lead or draw. The prefix "*e*," means "out," or "out of." To educate is to draw out — not to hammer in. This is based on the tacit belief that there is a wellspring of information, feelings, and thoughts in the mind of every child. Though some children will need no external cues to share these, some do. It is therefore the task of the educator to draw those things out of the child. Even in the secular world, that is deemed to be a philosophical truth.

In our world, *l'havdil*, this is certainly true. In the final chapter of *Nesivei Chinuch*, the Slonimer Rebbe writes as follows: "It is incumbent upon [the *mechanech*] firstly to know that in every child there is a sacred *neshamah* and a portion of the Divine from Above, despite that surrounding the child there is the hold of externals and hindrances [on him]. One needs to constantly search for devices with which to open his heart and mind."

One last point that is essential. A *mechanech* who deals with the non-active participant by ignoring him does a tremendous disservice and fails to fulfill his role. While such a child would hate to be forcibly hurled into a compromising verbal situation — such as being forced to answer/translate/explain etc., he would equally hate to be ignored. He is silently crying out for a gentle hand to reach out to him — something of a life preserver — in order for him to be drawn into a role of active participation, albeit in a manner that suits him.

After all, the child has an instinctive drive to be verbal.

BRICK BY BRICK

We live in a world that glorifies final products and the complete fulfillment of goals. In that mood, how is a *mechanech* supposed to feel genuine gratification from producing what is arguably seen as small attainments in a child's development?

One of the lesser known lessons of *Megillas Esther* is related to this and actually provides a powerful "should-be" directive for any *chinuch* or parenting manual.

When Haman was dispatched by Achashveirosh to get Mordechai, dress him in regal vestments, mount him upon the king's stallion, and lead him through the streets of Shushan proclaiming "*Kachah ye'aseh la'ish...*" he discovered that Mordechai had been in the company of his disciples, giving them a *shiur*.

The Midrash's account of the event (*Esther Rabbah* 10:4) varies slightly from the version in the Gemara (*Megillah* 16a), but we can dwell on what is common to both sources — the particular halachah that was the focus of Mordechai's *shiur*.

Haman questioned Mordechai, "With which topic were you involved?"

"With the law of *kemitzah*," he replied, making reference to the *minchah*-offering, which consisted of sacrificing a handful of flour solution upon the *mizbeiach*. This small handful — the *kometz* — which was brought in the context of the *"korban Omer,"* effected an appeasement of Hashem by *Klal Yisrael*. And while the Maharsha explains that the particular *kometz* to which the Gemara refers is not from the *Omer* sacrifice, but rather from a *minchas yachid*, the flour-offering of a poor individual, the crucial point is still one and the same: an offering of even a diminutive size suffices in appeasing Hashem.

Haman, unable to fathom how this could be, asked, "What was the *kometz* made of? Silver? Gold?"

"No, it consisted of a small amount of grain," Mordechai responded.

Haman, who although keenly understood that Mordechai's learning could potentially prompt Hashem to abolish the decree of destruction against *Klal Yisrael*, nevertheless scoffed and asked, "Do you think that a tiny amount of your grain can have more clout than the 10,000 silver bars I have provided to carry out your destruction?"

Mordechai responded that Haman's suggestion was that of a *rasha*, because material wealth is ultimately meaningless; in contrast, the performance of an even a small mitzvah (or, as in this case, learning about one) is infinitely more powerful.

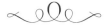

The perceived "smallness" of achievement is possibly delusional. Let's see why.

Logic dictates that the "building" of a *ben Torah* or a *bas Yisrael* can be likened in our minds to any traditional construction project. One of the similarities lies in that construction is done systematically: brick by brick, wall by wall. One cannot expect to create an entire edifice all at once, or even too quickly, for that matter.

But there is also another, more subtle, truth linked to this. Many years ago I contracted a company to build a small addition to our home. As each of the tradesmen came, did his portion of the project and left, I remember marveling at the visible *sipuk*, gratification, each of them felt. I, of course, was impatient and wanted to see the renovation complete and could not appreciate the aesthetic value of any single portion of the job in isolation. When I looked at the tradesmen, though, I realized that each had a keen sense of his own *tachlis*, his own particular objective, and each was content when it was realized. Each one took pride in his work. I grasped that it was my relative ignorance of the complexity of the entire endeavor that held me back from understanding the importance of any single component of it.

If this has truth within the context of physical construction, then it certainly has validity in the context of spiritual construction.

In a connected thought, we find that the *Sfas Emes* explains the downfall of Korach as having been rooted in his not realizing the importance of so-called "smaller" achievements. The singing of the *Leviim* thus did not represent a task of sufficient prominence for Korach; he aspired for more and actively pursued this aspiration — to the point of falling flat on his proverbial face. The higher one rises spiritually, explains the *Sfas Emes*, the more keenly he realizes the importance of each and every piece of the puzzle — not only the pieces that sit in the limelight.

Similarly, the more one comprehends the totality of *chinuch*, the more one is able to appreciate the importance of every single part of it.

In the *sefer U'Matzdikei HaRabbim Ke'Kochavim*, we find that the Brisker Rav, the Gri"z, was once asked a question related to the one at hand. What shall a *melamed* feel when he invests energies and efforts to teach difficult children, in light of the fact that one rarely sees any sort of blessing from the sizeable investment? The Brisker Rav answered that each and every recitation of *Kri'as Shema* by such a child, and every observance of Shabbos by such a child is to be regarded as a complete universe of achievement. The importance of even the smallest achievement in Yiddishkeit is immense.

In that same source, a beautiful explanation is offered for the Brisker Rav's statement. When it comes to spirituality, the accomplishment is by definition eternal. It is for that reason that there is no such thing as an insignificant achievement in *ruchniyus*.

So, Haman failed to understand this fundamental principle. The 10,000 bars of silver that he offered as an instrument of our downfall were absolutely useless, despite the inevitable fact that they gleamed and sparkled an awful lot and that they represented abundance and wealth. This was because money and all material things fade and perish, whereas the spiritual gain of something as seemingly tiny as the *kemitzah* is of boundless importance.

The upshot is that in Yiddishkeit in general, and in *chinuch* in particular, there is no such thing as an insignificant accomplishment. To make the mistake of thinking otherwise is to adopt a crass, goal orientation, which smacks, though slightly, of Haman's attitude.

Here are a few practical thoughts to help parents and *mechanchim* ascribe the deserved *chashivus* to what they might erroneously view as unimportant:

- Appreciating even the "small achievement" will engender a

desire on the part of a child to achieve more of the same and then to achieve things of a larger dimension.

- If a child has shown even a slight improvement, he must be recognized for it, for nothing breeds further success more than a self-image that includes success.

- Mean it. Children see straight through contrivances and ego-pandering exaggerations.

- Celebrate even small achievements with a *siyum*, a party, or a prize.

- Sensitivity needs to be exercised so it can be determined that expectations of children are realistic and not idealistic. This includes small goals; a child can be crushed by seeing himself as failing to fulfill his rebbi's or parent's dream.

There is no doubt that large and dramatic goals are needed to keep propelling us into further action and additional achievement. This goes for our children too. However, such goals cannot even be entertained without our first viewing the role of each component.

PART THREE

שְׁמַע בְּנִי מוּסַר אָבִיךָ... תּוֹרַת אִמֶּךָ

משלי א:ח

THE CRUCIAL ROLE PLAYED BY PARENTS

SINGING THE TUNE OF THE TEEN

QUESTION: *My husband and I have a difficult time getting through to our adolescent child. She is a wonderful daughter in almost all respects; but situations which require her to accept her parents' view become sources of contention, as she thinks she "understands better." How, as parents, can we deal with this and guide our children?*

As a prelude, I must say that the focus in dealing with this question lies much less with what a parent *shall* do than what a parent *shall not* do. Recipes are scarce and feeble, and a wise parent will best be cautious not to worsen a situation that might already be strained.

While I would guess that the so-called "generation gap" has been a challenge throughout time, the specific issue that is raised in this question has in fact become one of the most increasingly severe parenting issues of the age. How to relate to adolescent children is more of a concern in a complex society such as ours than it used to be when, at least on the surface, there was more stability and predictability in human behavior. Still, the teen years may always have been somewhat problematic.

THE HALACHAH

We ought to begin with a tell-tale sign of what makes the adolescent mind tick. The following halachah is cited in *Kitzur Shulchan Aruch* (143:18): "It is forbidden for one to strike his son who is a *gadol*. This stage of being a *gadol* does not depend on age but rather on the specific nature of the son. Any child who might be suspected of lashing back at his parent — whether verbally or in action — even if that child is younger than the age of *mitzvos*, it is forbidden to strike him. Rather [the parent] shall rebuke him with words. Anyone who strikes his mature child is deserving of excommunication, for he has transgressed the prohibition of '*Lifnei iveir…*' — placing a stumbling block before a 'blind' individual."

What clearly emerges is that when children arrive at a certain level of maturity, their self-concept can make them more rebellious and can even make them likely to lash out at their parents. This mindset comes with the territory. So, even during earlier periods of history, the scourge of adolescence seems to have been troubling.

One query that surfaces from the above passage is what the definition of "striking" might be. A cursory interpretation would be physically beating the child. However, based on two factors, I find that this interpretation is to be questioned. First of all, if a child is suspected of possibly lashing back at his parents "whether verbally or in action" it is probable that the concern is that the child might respond to his parents' methods *in kind*. If the son lashes out verbally at his parents, it is plausible that he has tasted the effects of harsh speech from them.

It would therefore follow that the same concern and the same cautionary warning pertain to when parents give excessive tongue lashings to children. And even if we read, "the parent shall rebuke him with words," the intention is that words should be the maximum of punitive measures — but even words need to be judicious and compassionate. The halachah is teaching us, I believe, that one ought to avoid a verbal beating of the child as much as a physical one.

In fact there is proof of this! In *Zriah U'Binyan*, Rav Shlomo Wolbe, *zt"l*, warns that shouting or speaking biting words of rebuke are more damaging to the recipient than something physical might be. The classical children's statement, "Sticks and stones… but words can never hurt me," is completely false. Words can hurt much more profoundly and indelibly than sticks and stones.

The upshot is clear. A parent needs to be sensitized to the realities of adolescence, and where there is contentiousness, a parent needs to maintain self-control and composure.

WHAT IS "MATURE"?

Now, what exactly do we mean when we say that a child has become "mature"? On the one hand we accept that a certain level of maturity has occurred when a child reaches the age of responsibility for *mitzvos*. Indeed, in halachah such a person is referred to as a *gadol*, or a *gedolah*.

At the same time, the Mishnah teaches us (*Avos* 5:21) that only when a young man turns fifteen is he considered the proper age to study Gemara. (Although it is the universal practice to actually begin teaching Gemara at a considerably younger age, the Mishnah means to say that the peak of those studies coincides with the boy's turning fifteen.)

The reason is simple, as found in the Rambam's commentary. Unlike Mishnah, which is straightforward, the study of Gemara requires intricate and analytical thinking, something which cannot be done with proficiency until the child is a bit older. Similar reasoning underlies the next statement of *Chazal* in the same passage. "*Ben shemoneh esrei l'chuppah*," eighteen is the age when a boy should consider getting married. This is because the required degree of responsibility and the requisite abilities in interpersonal skills have not adequately developed prior to that age.

The real issue, then, is that there is a gap between what a youth is in fact capable of and what the youth thinks he or she is capable of. That is the crux of the problem — and in fact is alluded to in the question itself.

In consideration of all this, the immediate objective is this: you need to both validate the child and at the same time convey a message of rank. Relay the message that the youth has indeed developed and has achieved maturity such that his or her views are worthy of consideration and respect (which in fact they probably are!), but that according to Torah (and *l'havdil* even according to secular laws pertaining to age and responsibility) he or she is only on the road to even greater wisdom.

PREVENTION

In terms of seeing what the source of the problem might be, I would argue that the way our children are raised today is a significant contributor to the situation. To begin with, the biological phenomena that transform the lives of youth are sources enough for confusion in our children, leading them to see themselves as adults when in fact they are far from it. (This explains the tendency that young adolescents have to seek to dress as if they were grown up.)

Other components figure even more prominently, however. The emphasis that secular society places on youth, the fact that the technological know-how of young people usually exceeds that of their parents, the mood of rights and entitlement that permeate contemporary living, the increasingly in-your-face style of today's speech and communication, the abundance of access and resources available to today's youth — these are the factors that exacerbate the task of dealing with adolescent children, especially if the pre-adolescent *chinuch* may have lacked adequate control.

The most fundamental component, however, is the spirit of parenting that is commonly found in today's world. Solving the issues of adolescent children lies primarily in prevention. When children are in the pre-teen years, the profile of parents must be such that love is tempered with reverence and that *kavod* is balanced with *yirah*. A compassionate and nurturing parent who also asserts his or her authority before young children, in the way that is prescribed by Torah, can be almost assured that the adolescent years of those children will be blessed: years of *nachas* for the parent and of growth for the child.

PARENTING: INSTINCT VS. SKILL

I often wonder why a task as intricate and as challenging as parenting is so often left to chance and to guesswork. Why do we tend to believe in our sense of correctness when it comes to the do's and don'ts of childrearing, when we would never dream of trusting that same sense when it comes to other things that are far less important? Just think of all the professionals and tradesmen to whom we turn for advice and guidance in the performance of myriad tasks. Then consider that we almost never appeal to the expertise of others when we involve ourselves in parenting. How does such an irony evolve?

Surely the most common justification is that parents were themselves children once, and they have vivid memories of how their own parents raised them. And insofar as most people consider themselves to be fine specimens of childrearing, they therefore have an implicit trust in the parenting skills they inherited. It is as the Gemara suggests at the end of *Maseches Sukkah*: what one says (and does) is merely what one has heard (or seen) in his parents' home.

So we are parents by emulation. The problem that emerges

from that thought, however, is that our parents (and certainly theirs) never had to deal with all the gadgetry, the opportunity, the imagery, the value systems, the technology, the moral decline, the accessibility and the complexity with which we as today's parents in fact must contend. Symbolic of the rapidness of change is, of course, the computer. So, talk about change! Before one has paid off his first purchase, his computer has already entered the netherworld of obsolescence. It is thus not very likely that the parenting techniques that may have been appropriate two and three decades ago have remained equally appropriate and equally relevant today. Parenting techniques may not have kept pace.

Another problem that surfaces is the historical legitimacy of parenting by emulation, in light of the fact that mankind's first parents had no parents of their own from whom to learn. If Adam and Chava had no models bequeathing to them a legacy of parenting skills, how did they figure out what to do? It thus stands to reason that ultimately there is another source for our parenting acumen.

There is no doubt, however, that when the *Ribbono shel Olam* created Adam and Chava, He infused into them a complex of instincts, which include the instinct for parenting. In the *Moreh Nevuchim* (in his discussion of the mitzvah of *shiluach hakein*), the Rambam mentions the maternal instinct, referring to it as *de'agah* — concern. Similarly, the Gemara in *Bava Kama* that discusses the law of *haba b'machteres*, one who steals into another's house, makes reference to a paternal instinct. So, while there may not have been infused into mankind a "filial instinct," so to speak, an instinct for parenting has been.

So, while we lack instincts to guide us in fixing cars, completing tax returns, and performing open heart surgery, to name but a few things — a fact that explains the near universality of relying upon others — we do have parenting instincts. It is upon these that we rely when we raise our children.

Alternatively, instincts are restricted. To begin with, they can come into conflict with each other. For example, what shall a woman do if her instinct for self-preservation is challenged by her maternal instinct? (It is worth noting that situations of such conflict abounded, *Rachmana litzlan*, during the Holocaust.)

And alas, based on empirically observed behavior, we know that instinct alone falls miserably short from being the source of prescription for parents. I will share four situations with which I or my colleagues, as educators, had to contend in the short span of one single week some years ago. (All names and venues have been changed.)

1. A teacher entered my office with a dilemma. Rivky, a weak student, was failing *dikduk*, although she was able to do reasonably well if merely allowed use of certain charts during testing. The only problem was that the girl's mother, even after she had been told clearly about the trauma that her child was experiencing as a result of being forced to contend with an unaltered curriculum, had remained adamant that absolutely no modification be made to Rivky's program. She did not want the child to be seen in a different light than her classmates. The teacher was afraid, and legitimately so, that Rivky's mother would be upset about the "modification" of Rivky's use of the charts during testing. I told the teacher to provide the charts but to desist from using the word "modified" on the test or the report card. (I reasoned that Rivky's sense of accomplishment from passing the test well justified the ploy.) What was at issue, however, was the mother's mindset. Why was her pride stronger than her instinctive drive to allow her struggling daughter a brief but comforting sense of self-satisfaction?

2. Shaindy arrives at school every day carrying her lunch box, like every other child in the fifth grade. What distinguishes Shaindy, though, is that most of the times that the teacher was able to check, the lunch box was empty — right in the morning. Shaindy, described as "skin and bones," was embarrassed to come to school without a lunch box, and would also make up excuses for why she preferred to "eat lunch" alone. But the lunch box was empty. *So what about Mother?* In truth, the mother is now a single parent, struggling with the financial burden of caring for her children. Now, the school and certain members of the community do help in many ongoing ways, but what was the mother thinking when she allows Shaindy out with an empty lunch box in the morning? Now, personally, when the teacher reported this to me I was loath to judge. That is, until I learned that Mother would be traveling to Eretz Yisrael with two daughters to spend Pesach there. Don't maternal instincts also establish reasonable priorities? Perhaps they don't!

3. Unfortunately, it happens that the lifestyle of some parents (often affluent ones) gets cramped by their parental duties. And rather than succumb, they fight back. So Yanky's parents decided to take the two-week skiing trip anyways — right in the middle of the learning *zman*. And they took Yanky with. Now that move, in and of itself, would have been errant enough (and it is curious that the Supreme Court in the U.K. in fact recently ruled *against* the right of parents to withdraw their children from school for the purpose of vacation, without the school's prior consent). However, when I considered that Yanky is struggling academically to begin with, the move falls into the genre of absolutely delinquent. (And that does not even touch upon the issue of *bitul Torah*, which is problematic enough!)

4. The celebration of Purim focuses on various things. But at center stage, undoubtedly, are children. When Yossi and his siblings were left with friends on Purim so that his parents could spend Purim in Eretz Yisrael, in my view there was a dereliction of responsibility at play.

I sincerely believe that none of the parents in the aforementioned scenarios acted with either malice or intended neglect. I believe that they want only the best for their offspring and act always in the belief that they are pursuing that goal. I do feel, though, that the proprieties of proper parenting simply elude many of us. Today more than ever.

The message that needs to be internalized, then, is the importance of rethinking the oft-distorted dictates of our parental instincts. We need assistance in analyzing our decisions — be it from *Rabbanim, mechanchim*, or from experts with other titles. And we dare not indulge in the hubris of "know-it-all-ism." Let us bridge the contemporary gap between instinct and skill.

IT'S WHAT FATHERS AND MOTHERS ARE FOR!

QUESTION: *It seems common for mothers to be more involved than fathers in the schoolwork/homework of their children. If this is so, ought it to be the case?*

To my knowledge there has been no survey taken, and no statistics compiled to justify the statement that mothers' involvement should, or actually does, exceed fathers' involvement. On the other hand, I have seen a measurable gender-based separation of tasks when it comes to the school-related roles of parents among many families.

One area where the separation of parental tasks is both encouraged and unavoidable is *chazarah* or other types of work pertaining to *Torah she'be'al peh*. As it is ruled by Torah that women and girls shall not learn Mishnah or Gemara, it is obvious that this will be an exclusively father-son category of study — one that in fact also promotes bonding between fathers and sons (besides its being the *mitzvah* of "*v'shinantam levanecha*"). Indeed, the older a son gets, the more there will be a natural tendency for father — as opposed to mother — to learn Torah with him.

Apart from that, however, the issue of separation of tasks among parents needs addressing. I feel that while it can be justified on some levels, it can often sow the seeds of serious confusion in a child.

Sometimes — but not always — the parameters of certain activities almost render it obvious that one parent, as opposed to the other, will be involved with them. Consider simple examples: baking a cake would be seen as mainly a female type of involvement, whereas fixing the backyard deck would likely be viewed as a masculine activity. And while one can surely conceive of exceptions even to these (consider, for example, the *Gemara Kiddushin* that tells us that certain Amora'im used to do household or culinary chores to personally prepare for Shabbos), many tasks are regarded as gender specific.

When it comes to parental *chinuch* of children, however, gender specificity can very well be ill-conceived.

I. SECULAR STUDIES

One of the common scenarios played out by *chareidi* parents, at least in America, is that Mommy will take an interest in, and perhaps help out in, assignments and homework connected to *limudei chol*, secular studies, whereas Tatty will not. Now, while this is not a place to discuss the pros and cons of secular studies in general, one point is self-evident: if a child is in a school where secular studies are taught, it is vital that he ascribe some degree of *chashivus* to them. It is therefore incorrect for parents to inadvertently suggest to the child that this part of his schooling lacks importance. Yes, we do wish to impart the supremacy of *limudei kodesh*, the sense that Torah is on an entirely different plane from *chol*, but, despite that, we must not suggest that any part of a child's program is unimportant.

When Tatty excludes himself from that portion of his child's education, he is sending a clear message: "This is not worthy of my involvement." The negative attitude that can result from an "only-Mommy-cares," scenario is such that it may be preferable for the child to be withdrawn from the secular program altogether than to remain in it with this sense of *zilzul* or *bitul*.

Alternatively, in order for a father to successfully avoid portraying derision of *limudei chol*, it will probably suffice for him to occasionally involve himself in them — perhaps those parts of the secular program that he might know best, such as math or science. Tatty can express occasional interest in the work, or actually assist with occasional learning tasks. He should visit the English teacher in addition to the rebbi at P.T.A. and advise his son that he is doing so. By analogy, a *hechsher* symbol need not be seen but on a small bit of the product's packaging for it to proclaim its unequivocal message of approval.

2. FATHER–DAUGHTER

One crucial area that bears special mention is the issue of fathers learning Torah with their daughters. We know that the Mishnah in *Sotah* (20a) teaches that a father shall not teach Torah to his daughters. At the same time, the *Rambam* (*Hilchos Talmud Torah* 1:13) and the *Shulchan Aruch* (*Yoreh Deiah* 246:6) both clarify that the restriction is limited to *Torah she'be'al peh*, and that there is nothing wrong with teaching one's daughter *Torah she'biksav*, the Written Law, as well as (according to other *poskim*) the areas of halachah and *hashkafah* that pertain to her development as a *bas Yisrael*. And the halachah in no way stipulates that a daughter may learn only as long as the mother does the teaching. Such learning can easily be done by father.

Moreover, there is a most inspiring pronouncement made by Hagaon Rav Michel Yehudah Lifkovitch, in his treatise on *chinuch* — *Darkei Hachaim* (p. 435). "It needs to be that every father take a portion and be a partner with the mother in the *chinuch* of daughters. The father needs to be concerned that there shall be a good connection with his daughter — no less than the mother's — and that the daughter feel a bond with her father, such that they converse about all matters…"

Whereas there will be a natural link between a mother and her daughter, based on the fact that, as Rav Michel Yehudah writes (ibid.), "*Daughters are close to their mothers in their actions and in their problems,*" the father's input requires a more concerted effort. With father being busy with more "out-of-the-home" types of activity, such as learning or work, there is not always the wherewithal to cultivate that vital relationship with his daughter. However, when a father gets involved in his daughter's homework and schoolwork, and when he invests in her development in Torah and proper *hashkafas hachaim*, he will have likely found the perfect venue in which to cultivate a *kesher* with his daughter, something that is necessary for her unfolding as a complete individual.

3. BASICS

- A mother's input into the complete *chinuch* of very young children — sons and daughters alike — is most vital, as she is more capable than the father of infusing into them a basic and fundamental level of *emunah*, as well as Jewish values and life skills.

- A *baal teshuvah* once asked me how he can make a valuable input into his son's learning, being that his son can "out-learn" him "any day of the week." I told him that plain discussion centered on learning, regardless of who is contributing more to the conversation, is beneficial. In fact, merely expressing praise or interest in the studies of a child can give tremendous *chizuk* to the child. In that sense, both fathers and mothers can further a child's development through these simple measures.

- Shlomo HaMelech labeled both *"mussar avicha"* and *"toras imecha"* as indispensable components in the upbringing of a child. And although there can occasionally be a blur in tracking the line of demarcation between these two orientations, I would suggest that there is one vital ingredient in the recipe, which can clarify the matter. When parents work in tandem with one another, when their efforts are coordinated and complement one another's, then the separation of tasks ceases to be a challenge. Yes, there will be certain things that are gender specific, but on the whole, both parents need to be involved in most things. That's what fathers and mothers are for!

THE PARENTAL PORTION OF CHINUCH
PART ONE: SHALOM BAYIS

There is an old anecdote, based on an intended misinterpretation of a famous *pasuk* in *Tehillim*. When it comes to either claiming credit for children's schooling successes or casting blame on someone for failures, what often happens is as follows: "*L'hagid ki yashar*" — When things go well, parents are likely to say, "*Hashem tzuri*" — Hashem is my Creator, my Rock and my children's successes are obviously attributable to the fact that I am rather wonderful, and I clearly deserve this Divine intervention in the achievements of my child. However, "*V'lo*" — when things do not go quite that well, then, "*avlasah bo*" — the fault lies in him, namely, in the *melamed*!

Although this presents a jaded look at the manner in which some parents fail to recognize the positive input made by their children's *mechanchim* and the fact that only when they seek to explain their offspring's possible failings do some give "credit," so to speak, to teachers, there is nevertheless a large measure of truth in part of the anecdote — namely the importance of parental input into the *chinuch* of the child, and the degree to which it can either facilitate or thwart successful *chinuch*. Parental pride in a child who is a paragon of virtue is actually quite legitimate. And though his educators could well be praised for their pivotal role in providing a job well done, there is also no question that such a child was raised by parents who were doing things right too.

The child who is not such a specimen of the finer virtues, however, must also be seen as the by-product of his parents' child-rearing skills (or lack thereof). One of the most renowned *mechanchim* in North America once said, "Line me up a bunch of children on one wall, and line up their parents on the other wall opposite them, and I'll be able to match them up!"

What he meant to say is that it is not difficult to attribute the deficiencies and shortcomings that afflict young people to their parents and to the parenting flaws that they displayed. It may be a somewhat harsh view of the reality, but I believe it is a truthful one: the Torah ascribes both good and bad behavior of young people to their parents. And while the blessing of good progeny is a matter of *siyata d'Shemaya* and something for which we daven, we still subscribe to the view that the nature of children is largely attributable to the *chinuch* they received at home.

One example of this — just one of many — is that Pinchas, the *tzaddik* whose pious zeal removed Divine wrath from *Klal Yisrael*, is *meyuchas* — his lineage is recounted in the text of the Torah and traced to Aharon. And as *meforshim* explain, it is to connect the actions of Pinchas to the legacy he received at home.

Another example is the fact that a *bas kohein* who acted immorally is meted out a more severe punishment than a *bas Yisrael* who committed the identical indiscretion. This is because, as the Torah writes, "*Es aviha hi mechaleles* — she has profaned her father [a *kohein*] through her actions." Rashi comments that this is because when outsiders look on at the entire episode they mutter, "*Arur she'zu gidal; arur she'zu yalad*," the parents that brought this girl into the world and raised her are cursed. The woman's misdeeds are linked to her parents.

Similarly, in *Kitzur Shulchan Aruch* (*Siman* 142) we discover the statement that the greatest show of respect to one's parents is when one acts honorably. This is because when onlookers perceive a young person who is admirable, they will admire the parents who reared him or her.

The premise that validates all these ideas is that parents are correctly credited (even if not exclusively so) with the unfolding persona of their child — both negatively and positively.

That being said, it is crucial that I pose the notion that parenting is essential to the spiritual, psychological, and academic development of a child. Alternatively, so obvious is this and so pervasive is parenting that it would be truly impossible to do justice to the entire concept in a single article. In future articles, *b'ezras Hashem*, we might deal with certain specifics. In this context, though, let us discuss a fundament that forms the veritable bedrock of good parenting: the familiar issue known as "*shalom bayis*."

Taking the approach of "negative identification," we present clear evidence of the way in which a lack of *shalom bayis* can impact upon a child.

The second and third topics related in *Parashas Ki Seitzei* are "*shtei nashim* — two wives" and "*ben sorer u'moreh* — a rebellious son." The first of these is a scenario in which a man has two wives, one of whom he hates ("*ha'achas senu'ah*") and how he might seek to transpose this attitude to the way in which he will bequeath his estate to their children later on.

The second topic is one in which a son has become irrevocably corrupt, rebelling both against his parents' words and against the Torah. Citing the words of *Chazal*, Rashi articulates the clear message derived from the *semichus*, juxtaposition, of these two issues. Stated simply, if one has a spouse whom he or she hates, the end result will be that their marriage will produce a *ben sorer u'moreh*.

The reasoning behind this prediction is crucial, for *Chazal*, I believe, appeal to basic human nature in formulating it. A child who is raised in an atmosphere in which there is relentless disagreement will end up lacking the confidence and stability needed for healthy growth. The character that will emerge from within that situation is one who will effectively portray a denial of that same "system" that is represented by the adult world and by the notion of "authority" that is associated with it. The *ben sorer u'moreh* is a natural consequence of marital discord. The corollary, therefore, is that for parents to raise a spiritually healthy child, they must maintain *shalom bayis*.

Of course, the most extreme manifestation of a lack of *shalom bayis* is divorce, the ultimate and total breakdown of the family unit, a situation that is unfortunately much more prevalent today than it has ever been in the familiar past.

We are told in the Gemara (*Gittin* 90a), "He who divorces his first wife causes the *mizbeiach* to shed tears." A terrible scenario indeed, but why is the *mizbeiach* used as the venue to symbolize the sadness inherent in the tears shed over marriage breakdown?

I once heard a beautiful explanation offered by Rav Avraham Pam at an Agudath Israel Convention. When a marriage terminates, as sometimes it indeed must, there can be severe impact upon a number of individuals. However, invariably, explained the Rosh Yeshivah, the greatest victims are the children, who will now be faced with trying circumstances at nearly every turn of their lives — from homework to Yom Tov, from the pre-school graduation to the *chuppah*. The children are the *korbanos*.

Now, as is known, the place for *korbanos* is the *mizbeiach*, the undisputed venue for sacrifices. However, even the *mizbeiach*, experienced as it is in beholding *korbanos*, cannot help but shed tears over the children of divorce, for the sadness entailed in such a situation surpasses all others.

Now, in order for me not to be misunderstood, I cite this comment of Rav Pam not to judge or cast aspersions upon those who have concluded their marriage — for it happens that such a dire step must absolutely be taken. The relevance to the context is simple, though: it is to illustrate the effect that a lack of *shalom bayis* has upon children. And even when a lack of *shalom bayis* does not reach such extreme proportions as a divorce, the victimization of children nevertheless occurs.

The exact definition of *shalom bayis* — specifically as it pertains to *chinuch habanim* — will be discussed next.

THE PARENTAL PORTION OF CHINUCH
PART TWO: THE IMPACT OF DISCORD

In the previous chapter, we posed the idea that there is a link between marital discord in the home and between dysfunctional manifestations possibly surfacing among the children who are raised in that home. It is worthwhile, however, to consider not only the reasoning for that concept, but how it surfaces on two planes of a child's life.

EMOTIONAL — LOSING FAITH

Emotional strength is vital to the vigor of any individual. The early years are when we instill this into our children.

As trite as comparisons to the tree might appear, there is obvious validity to this Torah-based parallel. We read, "*Ha'adam eitz hasadeh* — Man is like the tree of the field." This has meaning on numerous levels — including the one at hand. Consider the tender sapling first planted in a bed of soil. We often see that a young new tree is in need of a rod tied to it, giving it support until it takes root and achieves stability. This is analogous to children, for whether in the area of physical nutrition, spiritual guidance, or emotional security, a developing child also needs firm support in order to emerge with strength.

In the main, parents comprise that rod of support. Indeed, in connection with that fact, it may be not farfetched to suggest a link between the two meanings of the word *"shevet,"* a link that is based upon this premise. On the one hand, *"shevet"* denotes tribe, which is the symbol of strong and viable progeny. On the other hand, it is also translated as rod, or stick. The connection that is possibly connoted is that progeny can neither endure nor flourish without the strength of that rod, which signifies the child's support system as he or she is growing up.

The support system needs to be firm (although never inflexible!). When there is discord — a lack of *shalom bayis* — between parents, the rod is by definition weakened and rendered incapable of providing the support that is needed. A child growing up within a discord-filled household is prone to be haunted with fear that his or her support system is breaking down altogether and is unreliable. As a result of the shortage of confidence now present in that child, the process of his or her "taking root" will almost certainly be associated with a measure of distortion from the norm that should have been.

Some years ago, I chatted with a young man who had "gone off the *derech*," and I asked him what had precipitated his fall. His cited that there had never been harmony between his parents. This ultimately caused him to be skeptical of his parents' authority, and then authority figures in general — including his teachers and *Rabbanim*. He shared that he felt that the "system had failed him." So he failed the system in return. That story, *baruch Hashem*, had a happy ending: after a couple of years in good surroundings in Eretz Yisrael, the young man successfully navigated his own return to *Torah u'mitzvos*. But what of all those stories that sadly do not conclude on such a happy note?

So, even if we were to consider nothing but the emotional benefit of the children alone, we must conclude that marital harmony is an objective into which parents need to invest effort — even including seeking guidance and counsel. And although *Chazal* seem to have referred to *shalom bayis* as a *zechus* (see *Sotah* 17a: *"Zachu, Shechinah beineihem"*), there is in fact more involved than Divine assistance alone. I recently discovered a beautiful interpretation of Rav Eliyahu Dessler on the word *zechus*: it is related etymologically to *zakus*, purity. The suggestion made here is that even those things which we can rightfully attribute to *zechuyos*, or to *siyata d'Shemaya*, are in fact attributable to our own efforts at achieving purity and goodness in our lives. If parents actively pursue the shared agenda of inducing a pure air of *shalom bayis* into their home, then the Divine Presence will grace their home. That will then have the obvious and the beneficial impact upon the character of the children raised therein.

PRACTICAL — MAKING CHOICES

One of the areas in which marital discord presents itself to children is that of choices: of decision making and of identifying appropriate rules and principles of behavior. Regarding this concept, the phenomenon of "discord" that has a negative impact is not only the pervasive kind we usually describe as "a lack of *shalom bayis*." For this context, discord can also take the much more common dimension of *"chilukei dei'os,"* disputes concerning specific *shailos* or issues of lifestyle and *hashkafah*.

An imperative that is generally actualized within a healthy home is that the child will be raised with a single and uniform set of principles — uniform because it is drawn from the input of both parents. That uniformity is what transforms the child into a principled and consistent human being. The reason is simple: uniformity translates in the child's mind as something resembling infallibility. The *chinuch* the child receives at home thus bolsters the child's ability to make determinations. This pertains to everything from table manners to religious precepts and the vast area between. A well-reared child is one who has been taught about life singularly, together by the two individuals vital to the child's growth. Consequently he knows what to think, how to behave and what to say. It emanates from the fact that his parents have jointly furnished for him a trusted and solid complex of knowledge and beliefs.

Discord, on the other hand, will result in a child's possibly learning that there are at least two diverse approaches to life's issues — Tatty's and Mommy's. However, he will likely conclude that just as *one* of those approaches must be questionable and fallible, perhaps *both* are. In the end, as the child has probably lost faith in the views of both parents, when the time comes for him to decide on action — consistently and according to a single set of principles — he may well abandon both, by virtue of their diversity. But if parents are not making the decisions, who is!? By default, that role will be assumed by the child — and at a stage in life when the child lacks the experience and the wisdom to make crucial life choices.

A rather elementary example of this came up a few years ago. In one family affected both by specific *chilukei dei'os* and a general lack of *shalom bayis*, the father felt very strongly that his son must wear *chassidishe* garb, while the mother denigrated that idea. She imparted the clear message to her son that *chassidishe levush* was not important to her and that a *yeshivishe* mode of dress was perfectly acceptable. The child ended up abandoning both sentiments, and when the opportunity arose opted for a dress code that is decidedly un-Jewish altogether (and sadly in keeping with some of his other choices!).

A child will place little or no stock in his parents' set of rules and beliefs if those rules and beliefs are areas of contention between the parents themselves. In a functionally healthy household, if and when there may be a difference of opinion between parents about a crucial issue — as indeed there must be on occasion — those parents have a critical obligation to conceal their dispute as much as possible from their children.

Long ago I heard elucidated the notion that *machlokes*, conflict, based on the root, "*ch,l,k*," is the underpinning of "*hachlakah*," slipping, formed from the same root. That which causes a child to slip and to lose his footings as he or she grows, is an aura of *machlokes* that might permeate one's life. The Maharal teaches that the advent of *machlokes* in the annals of Torah, just prior to the period of the Tanna'im, marked the onset of weakness in Torah knowledge, a situation that ultimately precipitated the need for writing down *Torah she'be'al peh*.

Dispute and conflict undermine the confidence children have both in the people who are engaged in the conflict and in what they teach them.

The protocols of parenting are ineffective against a backdrop of a lack of *shalom bayis*. That said, however, we must know that even if *shalom bayis* is present, parents need to be skilled in order to raise children in today's world.

THE PARENTAL PORTION OF CHINUCH
PART THREE: "VITAMINS N AND H"

I n the previous two chapters, I primarily emphasized *shalom bayis* as the foundation of good parenting. In this final installment, the focus turns to a pair of key parenting components.

One of the most noted Jewish educators in North America, Rabbi Yoel Kramer, has spoken about what he refers to as "Vitamin N," a psychological nutrient that is just as important to the psycho-emotional development of a child as regular biological nutrients are to the child's physical growth.

The "N" stands for "No," an increasingly uncommon response in parental parlance. The reasons why "No" is seldom employed these days might vary. For one, some parents are somewhat intimidated by their own children, perhaps because their children are proficient in skill areas (such as computers) that may be new and too sophisticated for parents. Alternatively the phenomenon may be traced to the misguided reasoning some parents use, namely that to be a good parent one needs to lavish every luxury upon their children and to cater to their every whim. Whatever the reasoning, though, the results can be catastrophic.

A well-known passage in the Gemara (*Berachos* 32a) describes the defense that Moshe mustered on behalf of *Klal Yisrael* following the sin of the *Eigel*. It is actually the fault, he said, of the great wealth that was given to the people when they departed from Mitzrayim. They performed the sin of the Golden Calf because of the abundance of gold they were given.

R' Yochanan, in that passage, compares this to a story of a father who bathes and clothes his son, then gives him a pouch full of money and places him in a spot which is prone to the commission of sin. Well, in that situation, says the Gemara, "*Mah yaaseh oso haben she'lo yecheta* — What can the son possibly do to avoid sinning?" Misdeed is inevitable.

The message is that when a parent over-provides for a child, the child will be endangered by himself. The human inclination to stray is latent within all of us — this is natural. Yet, surrounding circumstances are the catalysts for straying. When parents furnish their child with all or most of what the child wishes for, they create the circumstances that cause the child to sin.

Indeed, this explains the common practice among yeshivos to limit the amount of cash they allow *talmidim* to bring to school. The reason is simple, and it has little to do with the enticements within the school itself (although, granted, buying too much *nosh* at the school canteen can be harmful too!). It is much more connected to the pre- and post-school activities. With money in his pocket, "Chaim" will be tempted to visit, say, the department store — or the corner variety store — to see what's available. (This is especially dangerous where children live in open and religiously unsheltered communities.) There they might explore things, and ponder things, and, next thing you know, they are determined to pursue those things as soon as they get the chance. Just one example of how excess endangers.

The absurdity involved in this issue is this: the essence of the child, on its most profound level — the *neshamah* — does not crave much of what he verbally asks for. In fact, as the *Mesillas Yesharim* explains (in the first chapter), the *neshamah* actually shuns it. In reality, the child experiences a primal sort of serenity that comes from knowing that he is anchored, and that his parents are lovingly monitoring him and his development and that they establish boundaries for him. "No" is what the *neshamah* truly craves, and parents need to cater to that sublime essence of their child — not to the base, external side.

(Obviously there are many occasions when the parental response needs to be "Yes." Excessive parental refusal can be abusive. This, of course, obviates the need for analysis of each request.)

In light of all that has been said, one must wonder what motivates a child to ask for those things that might conflict with the *neshamah*. Why does a child actively seek a "Yes," when his inner self craves a "No"?

That question brings us to the second key parenting component: "Vitamin H." Where the H represents "happiness," the suggestion is that parents are advised to provide for the child that which truly promotes happiness. It is exclusively when that is *not* provided that the child will predictably seek replacements. And those pursuits will usually be things that he erroneously believes, as a result of media and societal influences — and as a result of his own *yetzer hara* — will feed him his required regimen of Vitamin H. When the child does not have the "real thing," he searches for replicas. Something gnaws at his inner core, making him feel deprived. Sadly, however, when parents attempt to address that with acquiescence and offer the child every tangible pleasure he requests, that is, the replicas, the satisfaction that the child seeks is never even remotely realized in an enduring way.

When I was a principal years ago, I dealt with a boy — call him Moshe — whose parents are very well-to-do and extremely loving. Because of their high-profile lifestyle, however, the parents — especially the mother — were out of the house, or traveling, more often than they were at home. True, Mommy would telephone from where she may have been to inquire about Moshe's wellbeing, yet, those phone calls were next to meaningless to Moshe. I detected a profound sadness in the boy, which I knew might leave a deep scar, despite the fact that he always had plenty of cash and all of the creature comforts and luxuries that a child that age could want.

It was not long before Moshe began to stray — ultimately even to the point of substance abuse — and to engage in a personal struggle, one that has not yet finished many years later. Moshe was looking for that which he was sorely lacking — happiness — and, like many others, undertook his futile hunt in alien territory. Unfortunately, wherever we turn we encounter stories like Moshe's.

Parents are urged to establish a home ambiance that is rich and warm. And involvement in the child's life and activities is really only one of several factors.

Humor — simple enjoyment — is another. The story of the guest who visited the Steipler, only to find him on the floor playing with an *einikel* is well known. Laughter and smiles in a child's home life will safeguard that the child seeks his happiness in the home.

Music and song can be another factor. It is, explains the Baal HaTanya, the quill of the *neshamah*. Through that language, the subliminal essences of people communicate best. It is also one of the secrets to the success of the "*Derech HaMaharal*" schools. And it increases the joy in one's life.

At the end of the day, child-rearing requires *siyata d'Shemaya*. However, even *siyata d'Shemaya* needs to be deserved. "*Tefillah oseh machtzeh* — prayer effects half the result," teach *Chazal*. So daven — and then daven some more. But practice basic nutrition too, without forgetting to give your brood a regular intake of vitamins: Vitamin N and Vitamin H. And though they appear slightly contradictory, they are in fact viable only in conjunction with one another — in balance. And bear in mind that "balance" is what is most needed in order for a person to be… well, balanced!

PART FOUR

כִּי הִיא חַיֶּיךָ וְאֹרֶךְ יָמֶיךָ

דברים ל:כ

AN ASSORTMENT OF *CHINUCH* STANDARDS AND GOALS

LOFTY, EXTRINSIC PURSUITS

Several years ago tens of thousands of girls and ladies around the world feted the seventieth *yahrtzeit* of Sarah Schenirer, *a"h*, the mother and champion of *chinuch habanos* in the modern age. Arguably, Frau Schenirer had in mind a specific and precise concept of girls' education when she founded her Bais Yaakov in Krakow nearly a century ago. She surely must have had a defined vision of what *chinuch habanos* ought to be. A single individual, with a single dream.

Interestingly, though, if one were to inspect a sampling of Torah schools for girls across the world today, one would find anything but uniformity and single-mindedness. Whether the issue is language of instruction, uniform dress code, desired depth of Torah study, curriculum, balanced emphasis on secular studies, standards of *tzni'us* and personal conduct — there are tremendous differences, if not downright disagreements, between *mosdos* in today's vast Bais Yaakov network. In countless ways, the stark diversity makes an observer almost wonder: Can only a single stream of *chinuch* consciousness lay claim to the legacy of Sarah Schenirer, or can numerous streams all be heirs? If all are legitimate beneficiaries of her inheritance, there must be a common sense of purpose. What, then, is the core *modus operandi* of *chinuch habanos*?

One is reminded of a similar phenomenon of diversification elsewhere, that is, in the world of *Chassidus*. There was one Baal Shem Tov, *zy"a*. One individual, with a single vision! Yet that vision was supplanted by division, for even a cursory study of various groups of Chassidim today compels the viewer to ask if there is any unifying factor at all. Yet, there are aspects that are endemic to all *Chassiduyos*: those aspects collectively constitute the universal definition of *Chassidus* — diversity notwithstanding.

So is it arguably for Torah education for girls. We need to discover, then, what are the axiomatic principles fundamental to all girls' *chinuch*?

The starting point of analysis needs to be the query, "Why do we, as Jews, learn anything at all?" That *shailah*, insofar as there is a difference between girls and boys in this matter, brings us to the distinction between what we shall call "intrinsically worthwhile goals" and "extrinsically worthwhile goals." Something is considered to have intrinsic value if it is pursued for its own sake. Health, for example, is intrinsically important, for we need not justify its pursuit by saying that it promotes something else. Health is good in and of itself.

Alternatively, that which is considered to have only extrinsic value is that which is important only because it serves a second, and hopefully higher, purpose. Ownership of a car, for instance, has extrinsic value only (despite what automobile enthusiasts might feel). Its essence is that it facilitates transportation.

With this dichotomy in mind, we might understand the difference between some educational goals and others. The obligation to study Torah is intrinsically important for a boy or for a man. One need not justify the study of *Bava Kama*, for example, by saying that it will lead to a better ability to decide what to do when my steer gores your cow. "*Shor she'nagach es ha'parah*" is part of the sacred Torah, and it is the obligation of every Jewish male to study all of Torah. That sort of *limud haTorah* is undertaken by men for its own sake: it is intrinsically worthwhile.

Chazal have told us otherwise regarding Torah study among Jewish women. While the *Shulchan Aruch* does stipulate that a female shall recite the blessing of "*la'asok b'divrei Torah*" each morning, the commentaries explain that this is merely because women are obliged to learn the practicalities of Torah as those affect their lives, and not because there is a mitzvah of *talmud Torah* per se. So while Torah does need to be studied by girls, it is for the purpose of producing committed and observant Jewish women. And while the Torah remains an intrinsically sacred body of knowledge, its pursuit by ladies is of extrinsic value alone.

The upshot is that *limud haTorah* among our sons is not "goal-oriented." Its counterpart among our daughters, though, is. While curricular selections do need to be made for our sons by their yeshivos, in the ultimate sense they might be pointless, because our sons need to learn all of Torah at some point in their lives. Curricular selectivity for our daughters, on the other hand, is most crucial, since theirs will not be lives of Torah study; theirs will be lives of Torah living. Torah life and Torah study may overlap, but they are two different things. *Chinuch habanos* is aimed at ushering these girls into Torah life — and not only their own, but that of all of the Jewish people.

So, whatever girls are made to study early in life needs to cater to that objective. The directives and parameters of this type of education is thus targeted — more so than in boys' schooling.

Furthermore, whereas the promotion of *ameilus baTorah* is vital among our male progeny, and while *bitul Torah* needs to be portrayed as something to be avoided by them at all costs, neither of these notions needs to play a role in the educational lives of our daughters.

At a meeting of the *Moetzes Gedolei Hatorah* held in Europe during the 1920s, one of the luminaries present declared that the most impacting Torah leader in *Klal Yisrael* did not even wear *tefillin*. When the others looked at him in puzzlement, he explained that he was referring to Frau Schenirer. Much as the platitude that we have often heard repeated, *chinuch habanos is* the key to Jewish survival, and this, despite its extrinsic nature.

Or perhaps because of it!

Now, with the philosophical statement having been made, the need exists to define a practicum for *chinuch habanos*. Yet, that task is nearly impossible in consideration of the vast range of sensibilities and assumptions made by Torah Jews. A universal "Daf-Yomi-like" concept cannot work. A fledgling Bais Yaakov school in the American Midwest will not necessarily embrace the exact same detailed objective as a sister school in Brooklyn, just as there will likely be some variance between the *chinuch habanos* of Golders Green and that of Meah She'arim. Consequently, the plethora of educational issues must be dealt with in accordance with those sensibilities.

Should girls be engaged in an in-depth and exhaustive study of *Ramban al haTorah*? Should a significant amount of school time be allotted to a school play — or to conventions? Should a girls' high school provide enough secular study for secondary school diplomas to be granted (and for post-secondary schooling to be facilitated)? To what extent ought a school to govern the private, off-school-hours, religious lives of its students? Is mastery of *lashon hakodesh* an educational imperative? These are among the dozens of questions that are pivotal in *chinuch habanos*. Yet, these questions might also be answered differently — yet, possibly, with equal correctness — in different locales and by different schools.

Predictably, a *vaad harabbanim* or a *vaad hachinuch* will help decide what the charter of *chinuch* ought to be in each school, and these decisions will predictably match the *modus vivendi* of the community that is served by that school.

However, the single and most fundamental motif for the Torah education — in all communities — is the safeguarding of the future generation of *bnos Yisrael* whose Yiddishkeit is braced with *yiras Shamayim*, with practical knowledge, with integrity, commitment, and idealism. Nothing else may really matter.

THE PSHETL — A KEY COMPONENT

QUESTION: *Why is the pshetl such a vital component in the celebration of a bar mitzvah? Why has that become so crucial to the ceremony?*

A word of preface: While the father declares "*Baruch she'petarani...* — Blessed is He Who exempted me from the punishment incurred from this boy," the father is not exempt from the responsibility of providing proper *chinuch* for his son. The "bar-mitzvah experience" is one occasion when important messages should be imparted to the young man, if the experience is to prove meaningful to him. It's important, as the adage goes, to "keep the mitzvah in bar mitzvah."

To begin with, it is worth noting that "bar mitzvah," as a concept, in no way entails the notion of ceremony. A bar mitzvah, strictly speaking, denotes a boy's experiencing a passage into a new phase of life. Any joyous celebration of that passage needs to be linked to that concept itself.

Indeed, in some places — and not long ago — the *simchah* consisted of little more than the boy's being called up to the Torah and a *"l'chaim"* following the davening. Today's elaborate affairs, as enjoyable as they are, are therefore not necessarily integral to the rite of passage, so to speak. In fact, to the contrary: in extreme cases of overindulgence, the celebration can easily divert attentions away from the central theme.

One popular ritual practiced rather widely today is to have the *bachur habar mitzvah* "*lein*" from the Torah — either the full *parashah*, or a portion such as *maftir*. In some places, he recites the *haftarah*. Those *hanhagos*, too, while arguably beautiful, have little basis in the centuries-long *masores* of our people. The explanation of how the practice evolved — primarily in America — is in all likelihood that it was designed to link the boy to Torah. The merit is implicit exclusively in that intention.

The upshot is that every aspect of today's customary bar mitzvah celebration should ideally reflect that theme. The *pshetl* needs thus to be regarded as a prime instrument for the achievement of that goal: it properly bonds a young man to Torah. Let us see some ways in which this can be achieved.

One aspect of the bar mitzvah is clearly linked to the *pshetl*: as noted, it fetes the inexorable connection to Torah and *mitzvos*.

Moreover, we find a statement made by the Maharshal in the laws of *aveilus*, that a mourner — during the twelve months of grief following the passing of a parent — may attend the celebration of a bar mitzvah, despite that he or she may not attend parties or public celebrations of most other types. The *seudah* of a bar mitzvah transcends the restriction of *aveilus* in much the same manner as a *siyum* does. The reasoning is that the joy that emanates from our embrace of Torah is not suppressed even by grief.

Of special interest, however, is what we find in that context, regarding what defines the bar mitzvah celebration. We discover that a bar mitzvah is the feast held either on the day that the boy becomes thirteen years old and a day or the day upon which he says his *derashah*. While we tend to make the effort to ensure that these two aspects coincide, and we schedule the "event" on the so-called "*bo bayom*," it can often happen that the two will not coincide. It is important, though, that the day of the *pshetl* is held in the same celebratory light as the coming of age itself.

Yet, perhaps it is not the recitation per se that is cause for pride, as much as the fact that the boy has mastered a certain "*sugya*," a topic — usually in halachah. This feat required the boy to exercise substantial intellectual effort in Torah. That, then, is what explains the central role of the *pshetl*: the learning that is associated with it — more than the recitation.

As a matter of fact, that possibly explains the common tradition, practiced by many, for listeners beginning to sing soon after the bar mitzvah begins his recitation. It is not an act of discourtesy, but a demonstration of the notion that what is crucial is that the young man learned through the intricate thesis presented within the undelivered dissertation.

I have even heard a particular *Chassidishe* interpretation: the delivery is perhaps to be seen as little more than a performance, which, when executed successfully, might even infuse the young man with a sense of pride, which may in turn not be conducive to his development of good *middos*. The best thing for good character development, it would follow, is the humbling experience of having a beautiful *derashah* and keeping it in. (This seems to echo the famed dictum of the Gemara, "*mashtuka bi'trein*," silence is twice as virtuous as speaking.)

An alternate explanation for the *minhag* of "singing in" is drawn from the *mishnah* near the end of *Maseches Taanis*, that explains that on the fifteenth day of Av, the young ladies in pursuit of marriage prospects, would collectively present themselves in plain, unadorned clothing, as opposed to fancier fare, for the reason of "*shelo levayeish es mi she'ein lo* — so as to avoid the embarrassment of those who may not be so endowed as to be able to purchase such finery."

Similarly, some young boys are not as intellectually endowed as many others and are therefore incapable of handling the understanding of a lengthy exegetical piece, let alone declaiming it in public. So, in order to avoid causing them shame on the occasion of their bar mitzvah, the tradition may have evolved to interrupt the recitation of every *pshetl*, irrespective of who the boy is and of how wonderfully he can impress the crowds with his erudition.

(I recall when, many years ago, I was told to prepare a *derashah* to recite at the *kiddush* that followed my *aufruf* — also a common practice in many circles. Sure enough, though, soon after I commenced, the men in the *shtiebel* began to sing. Later on, however, when the food and drink had disappeared, along with most of the men, a smaller group sat me down and ordered me to say the entire *derashah*. Luckily, I had in fact prepared.)

At the other end of the spectrum, I once read an interesting account involving the Pnei Menachem, *zy"a*, during the period when he had been a *rosh yeshivah*. He was in attendance at a bar mitzvah, and the boy was called up to recite his *pshetl*. Adhering to custom, the attendees waited a few seconds after the boy began and chimed in with a rousing chorus, whereupon the Pnei Menachem motioned to the audience that they should stop the singing. He ordered that they allow the boy to finish the declamation.

Following the *seudah*, one individual approached the Pnei

Menachem and questioned why he had stopped them from singing. "Is that not a *minhag Yisrael*?" the man asked.

The Pnei Menachem responded, "Yes it is a *minhag*, but true *lamdanim* (Torah scholars) do not usually emerge from such *minhagim*."

The venerable *pshetl* thus has a time-honored role in the rite of classical Jewish passage. It also is a powerful source for several possible *musrei haskeil*:

- What is important for a young Jewish man is the investment of mental effort to properly understand Torah.

- Humility is a prized character trait.

- Consideration for others is an attribute that will ideally be cultivated in a Jew.

- The real cause for celebration when a boy turns thirteen is the special bond that he will hopefully have with Torah.

- Any bar mitzvah celebration that imparts none of this is sorely incomplete.

INQUIRE ABOUT EARLIER DAYS!

QUESTION: *The hanhalah of my son's yeshivah is placing less and less emphasis on limudei chol in its effort to increase the time of limudei kodesh. Though they are sincerely interested in producing functionally literate talmidim, they have all but eliminated such things as science and social studies from the program. How concerned should I be?*

The degree of concern one has is, of course, a personal matter, and it will depend on one's priorities. This might be also influenced by the specific Torah directives that guide one's life in general. There have been — and there currently still are — *Gedolei Torah* who negate the importance of *limudei chol* altogether. Others have prescribed a serious but limited regimen of general studies — that is, only as much as is required for the functional keys of life to be provided to children — and nothing more. Others still have a broader view.

Two things are clear in my mind, though. One, hardly requiring repetition, is that we must not equate *kodesh* and *chol*. The second is that the greatest threat of a school offering a weak *limudei chol* program is that it becomes a breeding ground where children pick up poor character traits. Ultimately, however, a secular-studies policy will hopefully be designed according to determinations made by Torah luminaries.

One aspect of the question, though, is particularly worthy of note, and it is to that issue that I wish to devote the remainder of this essay.

Although strong arguments can perhaps be made for promoting the study of science and some social studies — such as the goal of better understanding *nifla'os haBorei*, the wonders of the Creator — the case for history is different, setting it apart from other *limudim*. I refer specifically to Jewish history (although in some ways all history is intertwined).

THE CASE FOR TEACHING HISTORIA

1. Mesiras HaTorah

Years ago I decided to randomly test *talmidim* on some basic historical knowledge. I was startled with the results; but upon reflection I realized that the reason for the apparent "ignorance" was that these young people had never been taught basics of *toldos am Yisrael*. That is why about thirty percent of eighth graders questioned believed that Rashi and Rebbi Akiva were contemporaries, and why about half of the total thought the same thing about Rav Saadia Gaon and the Vilna Gaon. And though a *yeshivah bachur* will predictably know that an Amora cannot dispute the opinion of a Tanna, or that the statement of an Acharon is not as weighty as that of a Rishon, they will just as predictably know nothing at all about the historical parameters of those classifications.

How can we properly foster an appreciation for the *mesoras haTorah* without imparting fundamental historical knowledge?

Around the end of the Tenth Century C.E., the Jewish elders of Kairouan (modern-day Tunis) were contending with the alarming incidence of young Jews converting to Islam, *Rachmana litzlan*. They reasoned that if they could somehow demonstrate the authenticity of *Torah she'be'al peh* to their young, they could stem the tide. They wrote their request, "*Keitzad nichtevah haMishnah*," to the *manhig* of Pumbedisa, Rav Sherira Gaon. He responded with his famous "*Iggeres d'Rav Sherira Gaon*," a detailed listing of the *mesorah* of *Torah she'be'al peh* from its start until his own era.

Not only did this make a serious impact upon the Jewish youth of Kairouan, but the *Iggeres* became a key to imparting crucial historical information to Jews in all ages. Indeed, many publishers of *Shas* saw fit to publish the treatise at the beginning of the first volume. A well-rounded perspective on the Jewish past is a key to the study of Torah, it was felt.

2. *The Yad Hashem*

Nothing can be clearer than the Torah's own prescriptive statement regarding the study of history. The basis of Jewishness is our acceptance and appreciation of Torah and the revelation at Sinai. Yet, the Torah declares that the manner in which to build this appreciation is by inspecting the pages of world history. Referring to *maamad Har Sinai*, the Torah states (*Devarim* 4:32), "Inquire about the earlier days that preceded you, from the day on which Hashem created man upon the earth and from one end of the heavens until the other end: was there ever such a great event or has anything been heard like it?"

How can genuine Jewish commitment be cultivated in the hearts of our children without their cognizance of the manner in which Hashem has interacted with our ancestors and has intervened in our affairs to preserve us? Hence another directive (*Devarim* 32:7): "*Zechor yemos olam, binu shenos dor vador; she'al avicha v'yagedcha, zikeinecha v'yomru lach* — Remember days of yore, contemplate the years of one generation and another. Ask your father and he will tell you; your elders and they will say to you..." This is not a bit of advice; this is an instruction.

3. A Sense of Self

We dwell on the *Churban Beis HaMikdash*. We lament the destruction through the words of the *kinos*, some of which were penned during the years of the Crusades. We chant the words of *Av HaRachamim* on Shabbos to remember the devastation wrought by the Crusaders, and we commemorate the Cossack revolt of Chmielnicki at the end of Sivan. We know that the Rambam, born in Cordova, Spain, had to leave that country and later became the famed physician to the Vizir of Egypt, but the "how" and "why" are not often pondered. At the Pesach Seder we sing, "*She'be'chol dor vador omdim aleinu l'chaloseinu*," noting that the enemies of Israel rise up against us in all generations with the intention of destroying us. And so much more!

Almost endless information combines together to form our collective national spirit, a mindset to which every Jew needs to connect as he seeks to formulate a Jewish self-concept. There is no conceivable way for a Yid to connect himself to that legacy without first immersing himself in the pools of history.

Indeed in the text of *kinos*, there is a refrain, "*Zechor meh hayah lanu*," remember what we once had. Yet, this is a meaningless refrain if uttered by an individual lacking basic knowledge of what once was and what was and is no longer.

Ultimately, one of the strongest bonds between people stems from their sharing burdens and goals. This solidarity, something to which we aspire, is known as *ahavas Yisrael*. However, the aspiration is best served by outlining the shared heritage and the shared sense of loss. We draw closer to one another through thinking about the common burdens that follow us from our past, and about the common goals we have for the future. That requires the study of history.

Consider the words of the Novominsker Rebbe, *shlita*, in an address to Torah Umesorah's Planning Conference on Teaching *Churban Europa*, over a decade ago. "Far more important than the sensitive subject of '*Mah zos asah Hashem lanu*' is to have the young growing *bnei Torah* be '*mitz'ta'er b'tzarasam shel Yisrael*,' to have a feeling that as a part of *Klal Yisrael* they must shed a tear for *Klal Yisrael's* suffering and losses." Absolutely nothing helps materialize that goal as effectively as the study of history.

So, as far as General Studies is concerned, the matter remains subject to debate, and therefore subject also to the decisions of *Gedolei Yisrael*.

As far as Jewish history is concerned, however, regardless of whether it is studied in the afternoon or the morning, in the winter or the summer, in great detail or in less, I would suggest that history is not *chol*, but *kodesh*. It is a pivotal element in the bid to provide *chinuch* with *sheleimus* to our children.

GIRLS OF TODAY...
WOMEN OF TOMORROW

QUESTION: *My daughter's high school appears to be forever busy with activities that fall into the category of "extra curricular" — such as class retreats, chesed projects, dramatic presentations, choir performances, convention planning, preparing exhibits, and so on. I sometimes sense that she is in an extended camp program rather than a high school. When I hear that other schools offer much the same type of experience to their students, I wonder if chinuch habanos has somehow taken a wrong turn somewhere. Am I right?*

Actually, you could not be farther from the truth. Let us see why.

In a nutshell, the objective of *chinuch habanos* is qualitatively different from that of *chinuch habanim*. And although I risk being challenged or criticized for this view, I maintain that it is solidly grounded in sources that, compiled together, outline the Torah's traditional view of the roles of men and women.

The primary agenda of *chinuch habanim* is scholastic. The ideal for every Jewish male is twofold: one is that he devote his life to Torah study, a value that is commonly referred to as *ameilus baTorah*, toiling in the pursuit of Torah, as noted in the first Rashi in *Parashas Bechukosai*. The second, as the Rambam writes in his introduction to the *Yad HaChazakah*, is that one shall possess the vast knowledge of *"kol haTorah,"* all of Torah. Both of these related objectives are scholastic by definition as well as by nature.

Indeed, we also find (see the first *perek* of *Kiddushin*) that learning is advantageous because it "leads to proper action." Furthermore, we also find in *Pirkei Avos* that one's fear of Hashem as well as one's scope of *maaseh* should both exceed his intellectual endeavor as far as primacy is concerned. We also read in the works of the greatest *mechanchim* of our time that it is incumbent upon a *mechanech* to impart and entrench the *yesodos ha'emunah*, the fundamental tenets of our faith, to their *talmidim*.

Despite these things, however, the time-honored approach for men and boys has always been rooted in straightforward *limud haTorah*. When *mussar*, *chassidus*, and *hashkafah* are added to the regimen of study, they are in fact deemed vital "additions," augmenting, but not supplanting, the supremacy of classical scholastics.

The portrait of the learning objective of *bnos Yisrael* is painted with different colors altogether. It emphasizes a different orientation — and in many ways a much more fundamental one — a role that is based upon, and in tune with, the essence of the *ishah*. Considering that the woman has a vast and profound impact on her surroundings — the home, the society, and all of those who inhabit these — the goal of *chinuch habanos* is properly understood as being the preparation of *bnos Yisrael* to dispatch their tasks, to realize their goals and to provide the impact according to the blueprint laid out by Torah.

To substantiate this thought, let us first consider the ground-level statement made by the Midrash (*Bereishis Rabbah* 14). The story is told of a *tzaddik* and a *tzaddeikes* who were married for ten years and were not blessed with progeny. They parted, and the *tzaddik* went on to wed a *resha'is*, while the *tzaddeikes* chose a *rasha* as her second spouse. In due course, relates the Midrash, the *rasha* had been transformed into a *tzaddik* while the original *tzaddik* had deteriorated into a *rasha*. The upshot? "*Hakol min ha'ishah*," declares the Midrash; all is determined by the wife.

That paradigm is presented to us often. Chava is accredited with negatively impacting upon her husband and with introducing sin to the human condition. Alternatively, Sarah Imeinu, recognized as having prophecy that transcended her husband's, was praised as being the individual who safeguarded the religious integrity of Yitzchak and the Jewish people. (See the opening chapter of *Shemos Rabbah*.) Rivkah is depicted as having had a keener handle on her two sons than Yitzchak did and as having taken dramatic initiatives to ensure that the spiritual heritage of Torah be properly secured in the hands of Yaakov. In general, we are taught (*Berachos* 10b): "*Ishah makeress b'orchim yoser mi'baalah*," a woman has a more profound insight than her husband into the essence of guests, or of those with whom they come into contact.

While the wife of Korach is blamed for creating a misguided sense of ambition in her husband, the wife of his associate, On ben Peles, is accredited with steering her husband out of harm's path, undermining his participation in the terrible rebellion.

On the most basic level, we are all familiar with the *pasuk*, "*Koh somar l'veis Yaakov v'sageid livnei Yisrael*," and with the interpretation of *Chazal* that "*l'veis Yaakov*" refers to the women. Moshe is instructed to impart the message of Jewish destiny first to the women and then to *bnei Yisrael*, the men. We might not be familiar, however, with the interpretation of the Maharsha that "*v'sageid livnei Yisrael*" does not mean, "You, Moshe, shall tell the men," but rather, "*she* — the Jewish woman — shall tell the Jewish male." It will be the role of the women to share the crucial message of accepting Torah, of loyal adherence to it and of being a holy nation of *kohanim*, with the men in their lives. The Maharsha teaches that the groundwork for our Yiddishkeit was made into the terrain of the Bais Yaakov, the women of our people.

To be sure, one finds many sources that portray this concept. It all indicates that the ideal persona of the *bas Yisrael* differs from that of her male counterpart. It revolves around the idea that since it is women who wield this phenomenal power in shaping the world, the Jewish woman needs to become prepared for this. She needs to be trained in such a fashion that will facilitate her making the most sanctified, the most elevated and most *Yiddishe* impact possible. Scholastics per se will therefore take a back seat to the cultivation of skills that make the *bas Yisrael* into the master builder of Jewish society.

So, whereas an additional *masechta* and another "*Reb Chaim*" will be the mainstay educational agendas of her brother, a young lady needs to be equipped with a broader array of tools — such that will albeit also include scholastics too! — in order to prime her for her sacred task in later years.

That process of preparation reaches its highest point during a girl's adolescence. Yes, the high school and seminary experiences are arguably the most vital in ensuring the integrity of overall *chinuch habanos* and must therefore be well rounded to meet this criterion. Teaching *chesed* through actual endeavors is only one aspect; and note that it is not adequately taught by a study of *Pirkei Avos* alone.

Conventions offer girls the sense of being connected to others elsewhere who share the same vision of *kedushah*. Plays and choir presentations and similar projects teach social responsibility, organizational skills, and they actualize those oft-hidden and untapped potentialities in students. Such activities build character and bolster confidence. Learning halachah, *middos tovos*, and *mussar* in a multi-varied multi-dimensional manners can produce more of those life skills that will be necessary in later years, for such study applies the knowledge rather than simply teaching it.

So, granted, today's *bas Yisrael* must also have strong academic footings, as mothers, wives, and teachers of tomorrow's world, but to denigrate the importance of those so-called "campy" activities in a girl's *chinuch* experience would be to sorely miss the point.

THE CHALLENGES FACING COMMUNITY SCHOOLS

QUESTION: *Living in a midsized Jewish community, I am offered a choice of mosdos for my children. The community is small enough for there to be a couple of community schools which welcome children from a broad selection of homes, but large enough for there to be schools which are more selective and serve specific segments within the community. Which one of these types of schools is a better choice?*

This issue touches on what is probably the most compelling so-called "Catch-22" in today's world of *chinuch* — in particular in out-of-town settings (the accolade "out of town" referring to all communities that are beyond the greater New York area). The issue can also not be properly understood without taking a look at its historical underpinnings. What gave rise to the community school?

When *Klal Yisrael* was experiencing its worst devastation in its history seven decades ago, the realization was made by such

Torah giants as Rav Shraga Feivel Mendlowitz, *zt"l*, that the shards of Torah that would survive would need to be transplanted in a solid bedrock of *chinuch* on these shores. At the time there were no more than six "yeshivos" for elementary-aged children in all of North America outside New York.

With the remark that, "It would be no small accomplishment if we got an additional 50,000 Jewish children to be able to recite *Krias Shema*," R' Shraga Feivel founded Torah Umesorah. His goal was to ensure that all Jewish children on this continent would receive a Torah education. Hence, the advent and the ultimate proliferation of community schools in dozens of Jewish communities throughout North America, as no school could succeed in the stated mission if it failed to hold forth a broad appeal.

I am among the many thousands who attended such schools in their youth. Indeed, I feel profoundly indebted to the school of my childhood — a Torah *mossad* that endures as one of the finest specimens of Torah Umesorah's handiwork anywhere — for the foundations in *emunah* and in learning that it furnished for me. I have no statistics compiled regarding my own school or others like it, but I am nonetheless confident in suggesting that there are thousands of staunchly *Torahdige* families in the world today whose existence is directly attributable to the *chinuch* provided by such community schools.

However, what happened in my own hometown, Toronto — as in other similar *kehillos* — was that the Jewish population grew and with it the need for additional shuls and schools. Add to that the desire that many survivors had to establish schools that would "specialize" in a "not-for-everyone" kind of way. With a blend of parochialism, seeming elitism, and the wish to promote specific *mesoros*, additional schools opened their doors.

Here is where the Catch-22 surfaces. As communities polarized and as these additional *mosdos* opened, families began to opt away from the community schools in a drive for spiritually upward mobility. Parents who were products themselves of the community schools drifted away from their old alma maters in pursuit of more restricted types of *chinuch* for their own children. Ironically, then, the ultimate *hatzlachah* of the older and more established schools became manifest through their becoming increasingly unpopular among their own graduates.

The ripple effect, however, did not stop there. It can be argued that the success of the community school, in its bid to produce Torah commitment in its students, has always been contingent upon many factors, not the least of which is the presence of a nucleus of strongly committed Torah families as a prerequisite demographic base for the school's population. Without a cadre of these standard bearers of Yiddishkeit, the school's ability to influence its other *talmidim* becomes diminished. (We know that *Chazal* teach that one learns more from his peers than from his *rebbeim*.) It thus follows that the greater the "*frumkeit* drain" among the students, the weaker the school becomes in perpetuating the Torah lifestyle. Many community schools thus got weakened in this fashion and were transformed over time into more of so-called "*kiruv* schools."

Ultimately, this scenario, which has been played out in city after city, has resulted in a rather clearly defined *chinuch* dichotomy, one that pleases some but confuses others. The "*cheder*" type school has developed a certain profile which, although it might vary somewhat from one *mossad* to the next, has a measure of universality. And in a similar vein, despite a similar degree of variance from one place to another, the community school (often referred to as the "day school") is likewise profiled. Ultimately, the matter of deciding where to send one's child becomes reduced to simply choosing from a smorgasbord of educational goals and ideals.

While one type of school might promote a higher level of Torah learning and greater Gemara fluency, for example, the other might develop a slower but more skill-based approach.

While one type of school may appear to be more proactive in teaching *middos* and *derech eretz*, the other is perhaps more likely to promote a greater sensitivity to *masores avos* and *daas Torah*.

While it can usually be predicted of one type of school that it will offer a better program in General Studies, it may also be likely that the same school will offer more diversity in its *limudei kodesh* program, including such subject matter as Jewish history, *Neviim*, and *lashon hakodesh*.

While one type of school may be accused of promoting more closed-mindedness in its *talmidim*, that fact can also easily be defended on the basis of its ability to inculcate greater *kedushah* in them. It might also be argued that means of discipline will be diverse in the two types of yeshivos.

There is almost no doubt that all schools and their administrations would love to exhibit only desirable traits and to pursue the finest *chinuch* objectives, but I have always found that this all but impossible, and that there will be a trade-off of features. Parents must be realistic in understanding that no school will offer absolutely everything and satisfy all standards. Clearly, then, parents must prioritize their own agendas.

One can therefore no sooner answer the question at hand than decide for someone else whether a cola drink is better than a lemon-lime. Yes, the choice of a drink will entirely boil down to tastes and personal preference, while in *chinuch* the choice is linked to more objectively discernible aspects that can be debated intelligently. Still, at the end of the day, choices are personal, and when not traceable to taste buds, they will be determined by the priorities that have been adopted by the individual.

When it comes to choosing a yeshivah, the thing to remember is that each of the two categories of school may offer distinct advantages that might be lacking in the other.

One objective in the *chinuch* of our children needs to be mentioned in this context, though, and this is the notion of acceptance of other types of Yidden. The fact that tolerance is probably cultivated in a community school more than in a *cheder* may not be reason enough for parents to opt for such a school. Yet, at the same time, that difference in social interaction needs to be borne in mind. Children raised in a venue in which only a single *derech* and a single demographic group are held in high regard, at the exclusion of all others, are in danger of developing a narrowness of thinking which, despite possible benefits, can stunt the proper cultivation of *ahavas Yisrael*. Parents of children in such venues are wise to keep this in mind and to compensate for it by means of the home-based components of education.

Whichever the *mossad*, an imperative for parents is to compensate for shortcomings.

INVESTING LIFE ITSELF

QUESTION: *One of the greatest challenges facing today's Torah teacher is the need to make the study of Torah more central in the lives of his talmidim. Is there an easy solution?*

We need to commence by describing the source and nature of the problem.

Firstly, one reason that this trend is so challenging is that a child's emotional distance from his learning can be difficult to detect. A student will sit in class with the Gemara open before him, and he might even be listening — at least peripherally — to the rebbi. He might even absorb the lesson and do well on his tests. The rebbi therefore has no reason to suspect that there might be something amiss.

Moreover, the youngster may be cooperative and congenial. He may dress according to the proper dress code, daven with a minyan, obey the school rules, and show no external sign of rebellion. However, there could be a quiet defiance brewing deep within him, whereby all that he learns and observes is making nearly no impact upon him. Yet, because of the outwardly conventional behavior and the child's pursuit of normal academic achievement, the rebbi — indeed, also the boy's (or girl's) parents — have little reason to worry that something is awry.

This is a most contemporary problem, because it is grounded in one specific parental and societal trend that was nearly non-existent many years ago. In a word: "competition." Many elements today vie for our children's allegiance. Research has revealed, for instance, that one of the greatest homework dilemmas today arises from the fact that when a child returns home from school there is a vast array of activities, gadgets, and pursuits of varied sorts, which seriously compete with schoolwork for the child's interest and attention.

It is worth mentioning here that I am not even referring to the threat of Internet per se and the insidious influence that it can have on people: that issue is well-known and has been amply (though perhaps not yet adequately) discussed. I am referring to things which are not innately problematic, or which in fact can be downright wholesome and worthwhile. The problem arises not necessarily from the nature of any single pursuit, but rather from the increasingly large role that these pursuits play and the alarming ease with which our children access them.

Music is just one example. It can be a beautiful augmentation to a growing person's life, but when one combines possible music lessons and practice with hearing CDs, musical iPods, and mp3 players, together with the growing flurry of singers and their releases, one sees how a wholesome hobby can be easily transformed into a pervasive preoccupation.

And we certainly must not forget the other pursuits which today's "conscientious and caring" parent finds himself compelled to provide for his son or daughter. So there will be music appreciation, extra sports, martial arts, debating society, pottery class, "*chasunah* dancing" (the contemporary equivalent of ballet), reading club, and chess — not to mention the old staples of stamp collections and possibly ornithology! These, and more, all act as drains on a young mind's attention.

So when Chaim is expected to devote himself to "*Shor she'nagach es ha'parah*," or when Chani is called on to delve into the difficult Ramban, their minds may be traveling off to distant and seemingly more appealing pastures.

Thus, while there likely will be no telltale or visible signs waving any flags to the adults in their lives, the silent problem that lurks in Chaim and Chani is nothing less than festering and steadily growing disinterest. The problem, then, that faces today's *mechanech* is how he can safeguard that his *talmid*'s heart will beat as excitedly from his learning as from his extra-curricular interests.

There is a *pasuk* that receives varied focus but can bear another second inspection, for therein lies a key to a possible solution. "And you shall keep the statutes and the laws which the person shall observe and shall live in them" (*Vayikra* 18:5). Numerous thoughts and *halachos* are derived from the last part of that verse: "*va'chai bahem* — and shall live in them."

However, the Chiddushei HaRim suggests two closely related interpretations of that verse to shed light on our issue at hand. The first of these is, "And he shall truly *live* in them." This means that when one is involved in Torah one needs to invest his life into that involvement. Most of our activities do not require complete commitment and extreme enthusiasm. We are not called upon to "truly *live*" in those activities. In fact, as a result of their relative lack of importance, we are quite often discouraged from imbuing our lifeblood into them.

Not so, our pursuit of Torah and *mitzvos*. When it comes to these, we are enjoined, "And you shall *live* in them." They are worthy of our personal reserve of effort and energy.

The second interpretation of the Chiddushei HaRim places the stress on the second word of the phrase: "*Va'chai bahem* — and you shall live *in them*." One needs to ask himself which endeavors are those from which he derives a sense of vigor and relevance. Live *in them*! states the Torah — almost to the exclusion of other things. Life shall come from *them*.

The upshot of our consideration of these ideas is a clear message to parents and *mechanchim* alike. These ideas formulate an approach with which to deal with the challenge at hand. I remember a particular rebbi under whom I studied in Eretz Yisrael (today he is a prominent *rosh yeshivah*). When he would discuss a topic, a dispute among *Rishonim*, an interpretation of a *Tosfos* and so on, he got so visibly excited and worked up. When he proceeded to share his rendition of the *pshat*, he was aglow in joy and exuberance. The sweat was visible on his brow and his satisfaction with his Torah was evident in the smile on his lips. It almost seemed that nothing in the world could have possibly made him happier than the *sugya* which he was, quite genuinely, living.

From that rebbi, apart from the actual concepts of *lomdus* that I merited learning from him, I gained a profound understanding of the role that Torah needs to play in our lives. That rebbi "lived" nothing as keenly as he lived Torah; and that rebbi, when he was involved in Torah, he threw his very essence into it. Two distinct but obviously related and crucial aspects!

If the approach that is taken by today's educator is that Torah learning is somewhat sterile, that is, that it is an academic pursuit, complete with homework, tests, and reports, and that it is essentially similar to the other varied academic pursuits that students encounter in school, then there is very little chance that the Torah will spark in the student's mind any monumental feelings of commitment, or that the Torah will truly impact upon his life.

If, on the other hand, the student perceives that Torah so animates his rebbi — or his father — such that there is nothing in this world that can compare in its ability to generate joy, "*lebedigkeit*," and enthusiasm in the parent or rebbi, then the youth will have learned that at least in the world of those adults who are important to him, the world he hopefully idolizes, Torah is not just another pursuit.

The *mishnah* in *Avos* (6:6) teaches us that one of the forty-eight things through which Torah is acquired is *simchah*, joy. The notion of *simchah* in education is certainly not new, but I believe that in this context the *mishnah* is referring to a different sort of joy. This is neither the general sort of gladness nor the *simchah* that emanates from one's self-concept of doing what is right — though both of those are vital in their own right. The *simchah* in the *mishnah* is, like the other notions in that context, inherent in the learning itself. If the student is taught to genuinely feel that nothing can make one happier than his learning, then — and perhaps only then — will he acquire Torah, and will he be able to overcome the malaise that afflicts today's world of *chinuch*.

THE BAS MITZVAH "CULTURE"

QUESTION: *Our oldest child, a daughter, recently turned eleven, and we've begun discussing plans for the celebration of her bas mitzvah. What would be the proper guidelines for such a celebration?*

The issue here raised is a perennial source of confusion for many people, but at the same time an important one.

At the very outset it is important to note that many common practices have evolved over the course of time — including in the realm of *chinuch* and the *minhagim* that are related to celebrating the milestones that our children reach. This will explain the great variance between what is common today and what used to be the regular order of things. It will also account for the differences in the way various communities fete some occasions.

In Chabad, for instance, there is a *minhag* of celebrating a bar mitzvah almost as lavishly as the way in which we celebrate a wedding. Among other communities, though, the occasion is marked in a much more Spartan fashion. Among Ashkenazim, there are special celebrations known as a *"shalom zachor,"* and a pre-*chasunah* *"aufruf,"* whereas among Sephardim both of these are non-existent. In most circles, a bride and groom will not see one another for the last week before their upcoming wedding (and in some cases, much longer than that!). Yet, many Sephardim and some Chassidim have a time-honored *minhag* whereby in the company of guests, the *chassan* and *kallah* meet to celebrate their upcoming marriage — on the last night before the *chasunah*. So, in the best of circumstances it is most difficult to state a clear directive concerning the manner in which many occasions are to be marked.

Moreover, that is even truer with respect to a *bas mitzvah*, because that particular milestone was in the past never traditionally marked in any manner at all among *shomrei mitzvos*. That is, until fairly recently. Over the course of the last century, most observant Yidden have adopted some form of celebration. I would suggest that this is a result of the effective birth and development of institutionalized *chinuch habanos*. With our daughters having in some ways joined our sons in the learning limelight, there has grown a desire to celebrate a *bas mitzvah* almost as much as a bar mitzvah, as an expression of having reached a certain level of maturity in Torah learning.

Significantly, though, it has been argued that the *bas mitzvah* is an American Jewish invention, and one forwarded by Reform and Conservative Judaism at that. Though this precludes the idea that the *bas mitzvah* is due to the advent of the Bais Yaakov movement, it is possible that both factors have in fact played roles.

Most significantly, though, it does appear that a *"bas mitzvah culture"* has emerged among *bnei Torah*— although taking on quite different dimensions in different communities.

In some places, the shul has become the setting in which this "coming-of-age" party is feted, and presumably following a learning program in which the *bnos mitzvah* have been taught the basics of what this milestone means. Alternatively, Rav Moshe Feinstein felt that since the practice of the *bas mitzvah* celebration has no basis in Torah, it might be something frivolous, and in light of our obligation to respect the sanctity of the *beis haknesses*, he felt that the shul ought not to be used for a *bas mitzvah* party any sooner that it would be used for any other birthday party, as the *seudah* is clearly not a *seudas mitzvah*. (See *Igros Moshe, Orach Chaim*, part 1, *siman* 104.)

(It should also be noted that Rav Moshe felt that the way in which we fete even the *bar mitzvah* has also gotten out of hand, remarking that he would abolish most of it if he could.)

In the school with which I used to be affiliated, we instituted a year-long in-school bas-mitzvah program for our sixth graders. Each month, the girls would focus on specific theme. They would learn a specific area of halachah (for example, the *halachos* of *hafrashas challah*) or *hashkafah* (such as the topic of *kevudah bas Melech penimah*.) The learning would involve various venues — frontal teaching by *morah*s, special presentations, guest *shiurim*, hands-on projects, and more. The ten-month program would culminate with an elegant but moderate class banquet to which mothers and grandmothers were invited.

In tandem with that we would gently discourage additional, private *bas mitzvah* celebrations; however, cognizant of the fact that most mothers would want to celebrate the event individually, we allowed that but set down strict guidelines for what was acceptable according to the school.

Such school-based programs are probably the best route to take, as they ensure at least that the celebration will be meaningful. What is of utmost importance, assuming that each family is part of a broader *kehillah*, is that the individual should not depart from the standard of that community, at least not in the direction of a more conspicuous celebration.

In many circles, the milestone is marked by little more than a family get-together. Consequently, there can be no clear directive regarding the *bas mitzvah*. All one can do in this venue is discuss the matter in general terms. It does make sense that one should adhere to the norm within one's *kehillah*. In light of that, then, the fundamental question that needs to be addressed is this: Why is it in fact that the *bas mitzvah* who is now obligated in *mitzvos* does not warrant the same attention as the bar mitzvah?

I have discovered two explanations for this. The first is in yet another *teshuvah* of Rav Moshe Feinstein (see *Igros Moshe, Orach Chaim*, part 2, *siman* 96). "In my humble view," writes Rav Moshe, "the difference is the result of the fact that there is no noticeable change in the practical observances of a girl when she becomes a *gedolah* (a halachic adult) from when she was still a *ketanah* (a halachic minor). This is different from the case of a boy, for whom the difference is clear: he can be part of a minyan and a *mezuman*, for when there is no discernible difference there is no *seudas mitzvah*."

In a similar vein, we discover the words of the *Lev Simchah*. The word "*bar*" in "bar mitzvah" also denotes something outward (as in the expression "*tocho k'baro* — one's inner essence jives with his outer appearance"). When a boy comes of age he becomes a member of the community; he is now able to make a halachically recognized impact upon others. His Jewish essence, so to speak, now bespeaks an outward impact. The *bar mitzvah*'s focus is thus outward, unlike the focus of the *bas* mitzvah, which is inward. Thus the former is celebrated while the latter is not.

In fact, that brings us to the second explanation for why a girl's Torah maturation is not recognized by the Torah. Years ago, the community of *mechanchim* in Toronto had the privilege of hearing the Lakewood Mashgiach, Rav Mattisyahu Salomon address them and answer questions on various *chinuch*-related topics. When the topic of *bas mitzvah* surfaced, he shared that he had once asked one of the *Gedolei Eretz Yisrael* — it might have been either the Chazon Ish or the Steipler — to explain this very phenomenon, which is our topic at hand. The answer he received was that what is being taught to a young lady when she is initiated into the world of *mitzvos* is that she must further refine and develop her *tznius*, modesty, and that agenda is arguably undermined through lavish celebrations. Something modest, within the context of family, might be in order, however.

Stated otherwise, the substance of the *simchah* is that we celebrate the spiritual plateau reached at that milestone. That may call for anything but a party. Even a lack of a celebration can thus comprise the most appropriate celebration, as may be the case with twelve-year-old girls.

So, paraphrasing the popular adage, we need to ensure that we keep the "mitzvah" in both "*bas mitzvah*" and "*bar mitzvah*."

A VOCATION UNLIKE ALL OTHERS

QUESTION: *My son has been in kollel for several years and is considering making a move into the workforce. He is considering going into chinuch and is seeking my guidance in the matter. In light of the well-known fact that people in chinuch often lead challenging lives, I am at a loss. What should I tell him?*

Before proceeding to the actual answer, I dare not miss the opportunity of pointing out a misnomer. The inadvertent suggestion made by the wording of this question is that learning in *kollel* is not really considered being part of the so-called "workforce." We perhaps need to be reminded that a young man who properly lives up to the rigors of *kollel* works harder than do most others. Now, that being said, we can proceed to the question at hand.

At the outset we need to consider *chinuch* as a task, as opposed to *chinuch* as a profession. My contention has always been that inadvertently we are in *chinuch* whether we are cognizant of it or not. At the beginning of *Avos*, the Mishnah urges us, "*V'ha'amidu talmidim harbeh* — And establish many disciples." We must assume that these words are not addressed only to those whose vocational choice puts them into an actual classroom. The conclusion to be drawn, then, is that we all do become educators in some way.

Again, in the morning *birchos Krias Shema*, we ask Hashem to infuse into our hearts the wisdom "*lilmod u'lelamed* — to learn and to teach." But if so few actually go on to teach, why is that request uttered with such universality? The answer, again, is that we will all be educators in some fashion.

Some will achieve this in the course of being parents, some professionally in a school setting, and others still by merely impacting on their surroundings. What's more is that insofar as we Jews have the capacity of strengthening and enhancing the world around us with Torah, being *mechanchim* comes to us naturally.

The idea that we are all grassroots *mechanchim* is further borne out by the tendency for parents — as appreciative as they might be of their children's *mechanchim* — to have clear views of what should and should not be done in the classroom. Whereas only a brazen few express views about the way that surgery — or filing income tax returns — or mending trousers — needs to be done, everyone is a self-proclaimed *maven* when it comes to *chinuch*. This is because everyone is in fact a *mechanech*. This is not meant to be derisive but rather to underscore the fact that instinctively we are educators.

Therefore, it is not the activity itself that is being questioned here, but rather the notion of choosing this activity to be a mode of *parnassah*.

Rav Yaakov Weinberg told me many years ago that *chinuch* is perhaps the only vocational choice which, if you have any doubts about whether or not it's for you, you should probably opt for something else. I understood his directive in this way: becoming a *mechanech* should be the result of an inner calling and nothing else. One's decision to go into *chinuch* needs to be derived from his sense that this is what beckons to him most.

One who chooses to go into *chinuch* professionally will thus be reinforced by this vision. That being said, a realistic perspective is worthwhile too. It is vital that prospective candidates know certain things about *chinuch*. Here are a few examples:

- A *mechanech* needs to be ready to be regarded by many others as someone who doesn't "really work." Such factors as lesson preparation, marking and extra-curricular responsibilities do not meet the common person's gaze, let alone the demands of the classroom itself.

- A *mechanech* is wise not to consider *chinuch* for the financial promise it offers, lest he be devastated in short order by significant disappointment (and that is assuming his or her being paid on time).

- A *mechanech* — and perhaps in this respect he is alone among professionals — must expect to be asked by friends ten years after he entered the field of *chinuch*, "So, are you still teaching?" (Imagine asking an attorney whether or not he still practices law!) In the eyes of some, being in *chinuch* is regarded as a temporary condition, not entirely unlike measles.

- A *mechanech* needs to know that his proficiency may be assessed by approximately one hundred people — *talmidim*, parents, administrators and assorted others all at the same time!

There is perhaps more on this, let us say, cautionary side of the equation. However, let us examine the positives.

Consider the fundamental truth that this life, by definition, entails toil and struggle. The well-known *pasuk* in *Iyov* (5:7), "*Ki adam l'amal yulad* — Man was born to toil," points to this inescapable reality. The only thing that sometimes appears to lie within our control, though, is the choice of the specific toil and struggle.

Let us consider that Shlomo HaMelech cautions us (*Koheles* 1:3), "*Mah yisron la'adam b'chol amalo she'yaamol tachas hashamesh* — What advantage is there unto man for all his toil under the sun?" In a sweeping statement, the wisest of men states that we will ultimately gain precious little, if anything at all, from all of our various pursuits — including obviously our vocations — that are "under the sun."

Midrash Rabbah on that *pasuk* relates the words of Rav Yudan to clarify: under the sun, man indeed will obtain no advantage from his endeavors; however "*lema'alah min hashemeh yesh lo*," from those pursuits that are regarded as above the sun, man will indeed reap genuine reward. The choice, then, is made simple enough: one may wisely seek the kinds of benefits that are of real value and that truly endure. Alternatively, one wastes his time by opting for pursuits that are deemed "under the sun," that is, this-worldly and material by nature. True merit is inherent only in such pursuits that are "beyond the sun," that is, spiritual by nature.

How fortunate, then, are those individuals who use this bit of information as a guiding light in their lives and who seek those toils and struggles that are on an other-worldly plateau. *Mechanchim* are among the elite of individuals who do.

I ought also to paraphrase the words of the previous Vizhnitzer Rebbe of Bnei Brak. He said, "One who does not observe Shabbos is not merely forfeiting his bit of *olam haba*: he is also missing his real *olam hazeh!*" In like fashion, notwithstanding the fiscal challenges that Torah educators tend to face, I can personally attest that few pleasures of this world compare with the gratification that comes from teaching and all it entails: imparting knowledge, contributing to a youth's personal development, imbuing *talmidim* with heightened *ruchniyus*, developing a personal bond with *talmidim*, serving as a link in a *mesorah* chain that began at Sinai. Quite apart from the other-worldly benefits to which Shlomo HaMelech was referring, there is a personal satisfaction truly sublime from a life of *chinuch*.

I have been at gatherings and conventions of various sorts over the years. These functions are all predicated upon people gathering for a purpose that is *l'sheim Shamayim* and devoted to the service of Yiddishkeit. I must say, however, that the elation and *sipuk hanefesh* that visibly adorn the faces of Torah educators at something like a Torah Umesorah Convention are surpassed by nothing else. The disadvantages of their chosen field come out in the wash, and what is left is something unparalleled for its level of contentment and *simchas hachaim*.

So, only one bit of guidance can be expressed to a person contemplating a move into the classroom, and it comes in the form of a question: What is it that you seek in life? For many, the response will be akin to what has been here described. And for them, their vocational choice — unless they fight it — thus becomes automatic.